CONNECTING
EMOTIONAL
INTELLIGENCE
TO THE
ONLINE
CLASSROOM

**MONITA LEAVITT AND
KIRSTEN STEIN**

FOREWORD BY LJILJANA KRNETA

Johns Hopkins University l

BALTIMORE

© 2025 Johns Hopkins University Press
All rights reserved. Published 2025
Printed in the United States of America on acid-free paper
2 4 6 8 9 7 5 3 1

Johns Hopkins University Press
2715 North Charles Street
Baltimore, Maryland 21218
www.press.jhu.edu

Library of Congress Cataloging-in-Publication Data is available.
A catalog record for this book is available from the British Library.

ISBN 978-1-4214-5221-0 (paperback)
ISBN 978-1-4214-5222-7 (ebook)

Special discounts are available for bulk purchases of this book.
For more information, please contact Special Sales at specialsales@jh.edu.

EU GPSR Authorized Representative
LOGOS EUROPE, 9 rue Nicolas Poussin, 17000, La Rochelle, France
E-mail: Contact@logoseurope.eu

Contents

Foreword, by LJILJANA KRNETA   vii

Acknowledgments   ix

1. Transitioning to Online Learning   1
2. Connecting Teachers with Students
   and Parents Online   15
3. Fostering a Supportive Virtual Classroom   37
4. Engaging Students as Active Online Learners   58
5. Assessing Academic and Emotional Progress
   in Online Learners   74
6. Involving Parents in the Virtual Learning Experience   93
7. Supporting Inclusivity in Online Teaching   110
8. Recognizing the Challenges of Online Teaching   122
9. Empowering Emotional Intelligence in Today's
   Virtual Classroom   138

References   155

Index   175

Foreword

THIS BOOK, *Connecting Emotional Intelligence to the Online Classroom*, by Monita Leavitt and Kirsten Stein, makes a valuable contribution to the field of virtual education, especially in a time that increasingly calls for the integration of emotional intelligence in the digital classroom. Their work offers an original and sophisticated approach to implementing emotional intelligence in the educational process, with a special focus on students' mental health, self-regulated learning skills, and emotional connection in the online environment.

The structure of the book, organized in nine units, enables a multilayered view of the topic, making it a useful resource for the modernization and improvement of the teaching process. One of the most prominent aspects of this work is its emphasis on the role of emotions in the process of self-regulated learning, which is essential for pedagogical and didactic methods. The authors point to the importance of emotions as a key component of learning—a topic that is rarely addressed in the existing literature on the relationship between emotions and cognition.

The concept woven throughout the book is that communication that encourages emotional intelligence contributes to a more dynamic and engaging learning process that activates all participants in virtual education. The authors address the challenges of online teaching by integrating their expertise, experience, and the specific needs of digital education, offering clear and precise instructions for creating an optimal environment in the online classroom. They elegantly link the theoretical foundation of emotional intelligence, as outlined by Daniel Goleman, with practical tools, providing comprehensive guidance for establishing a supportive climate in the online classroom; improving communication among students, teachers, and parents; and addressing the unique challenges of online education.

Among the special contributions of this book are the tools and guidelines for developing socio-emotional skills, as well as the book's rich bibliography, which points to further resources for anyone interested in this area. The authors also provide space for a critical review of individual approaches to inclusion in the virtual classroom, emphasizing teachers' flexibility and ability to respond to the different psychological needs of students. This approach further deepens the connection between teachers and students, as well as partnerships with parents, creating the foundation for inclusive and holistic education in an online environment.

Connecting Emotional Intelligence to the Online Classroom does not neglect issues of online safety, the importance of clear and accessible communication, and the need for active listening and dialogue. It emphasizes the importance of mutual respect and support in learning, thereby setting the standard for an emotionally connected and supportive environment in the virtual classroom. In contemporary literature, this book stands out for its comprehensive approach, inspirational content, and practical guidance.

I highly recommend this book to all pedagogues, psychologists, teachers, and parents of students who are interested in improving education through the integration of emotional intelligence in the teaching process. This valuable and inspiring work significantly contributes to a holistic approach to education in the digital age.

DR. LJILJANA KRNETA

President of the Association Together in Europe
(Banja Luca, Bosnia and Herzegovina),
University Professor, and
Research Psychologist

Acknowledgments

WITH GRATITUDE to our students near and far who have shown us the importance of nurturing emotional intelligence in virtual learning environments. You inspire us!

We want to express our deepest appreciation to Kathy Brammeier and Emma Stein for their help and support. This book's completion could not have been realized without you.

The world is a better place thanks to teachers who care about their students' emotional well-being. Thank *you*!

Connecting Emotional Intelligence to the Online Classroom

CHAPTER 1

Transitioning to Online Learning

Even with the unique challenges of online learning, I have seen the power of connection between students and teachers. My children have benefited from online teachers who ask meaningful questions, support their individual goals, and celebrate their successes. In my own teaching, I work to convey compassion, model curiosity, and encourage creativity. Through this work, I have found that my students are more open, eager, and motivated to learn.

—SYDNEY MILLER MILBERT, online educator and parent

Teaching and Learning in a Wired World

Today's teachers face unprecedented challenges as they strive to imagine and create a new culture of teaching and learning in the current wired world. To support their students' academic and social-emotional development, K–12 teachers are seeking ways to actively engage online learners and build classroom relationships. This book is designed for dedicated, challenged, and growth-oriented educators—whether they conduct online education in public schools, private schools, or other educational or independent settings, and whether they are new to teaching, transitioning from face-to-face classrooms, or creating blended classrooms.

Now more than ever, for meaningful and sustainable learning to take place, teachers need to address emotional intelligence (EI) in online classrooms to educate children in a safe, welcoming, and inclusive environment. This book draws heavily on academic research on emotional intelligence and learning, as well as on the authors' own online classroom experiences. It presents evidence on the value of including EI in online education and provides strategies and ideas for doing so, including specific teaching tips at the end of each chapter. This chapter and those that follow are meant to give teachers the information and tools they need to integrate emotional intelligence into online teaching to educate the whole child for academic, personal, and interpersonal success.

Incorporating Emotional Intelligence in the Online Classroom

Teachers are the primary facilitators of student learning in schools. Because each child is different and has a unique relationship to the world around them, educators need to be ready to provide support and guidance in a number of ways. Despite differences in age, predispositions, priorities, experiences, and environments, students think, feel, and connect with their social and physical settings when teachers show them support and present them with opportunities (Immordino-Yang et al. 2018). In such cases, a teacher's role shifts from a dispenser of knowledge to one of facilitator—someone who assists students in understanding, learning, and remembering while also helping them solve problems, take intellectual risks, and form relationships in the classroom. To promote both academic and social-emotional growth, teachers must be aware of the interests, as well as ability levels, of their students, and they must employ different strategies and techniques to meet individual needs. In a remote-learning setting, however, where in-person instruction and peer interactions may not be available, teachers can find it challenging to get to know their students, forge bonds, and build meaningful relationships with them.

Teachers and students who transitioned to a virtual environment during the COVID-19 pandemic experienced this difficulty. We know that building meaningful teacher-student relationships is critical to developing strong student engagement in educational environments (Mărgăriţoiu 2020), and research shows that high levels of student engagement, or active learning, allows students to thrive (Minshew 2019; Mugilan et al. 2021). Consequently, educators who teach online need to understand how to promote active learning in their online classrooms.

According to Darwish (2021), teachers bring two essential components to the classroom: (1) their experience and competence in the subject matter and (2) their knowledge of teaching strategies and methodology. To make learning more engaging and to encourage students to be more creative, motivated, and willing to take intellectual risks, teachers need to instill emotional intelligence in both of these components. Emotional connectivity is important not only to enable effective learning but also to cultivate the love of learning in students (Darwish 2021; Vejayaratnam et al. 2023). Thus, online teachers must engage students by creating a virtual environment that uses emotional intelligence to encourage personal learning and growth to take place.

The Rise of Virtual Learning

Anytime, anywhere technologies can enhance the learning experiences of students of all ages. These technologies can also bring the classroom into the home in ways that are academically productive (Watkins 2009). Although virtual learning was new to many teachers and students at the start of the pandemic, its expansion was part of an ongoing trend. Between 2000 and 2012, the global online learning industry exploded, growing by a massive 900% (Wildi-Yune and Cordero 2015). As brick-and-mortar spaces closed during the pandemic, schools had to offer distance, remote, or virtual learning through e-learning, online, or hybrid (blended learning) classes. As a result, the rapid and resilient growth that took place before the pandemic has spread to a greater range of school environments and geographic locations.

Remote learning trends from the beginning of COVID-19 to 2022 show that 4.6 million students at public institutions in the United States were offered a distance education course; 3 million of those students participated in at least one such course. Many online learning programs offered unique courses that were not found elsewhere (Vlasova 2022). Public and private schools realized the traditional way of educating children was not working, and many school districts were forced to change the way they approached education, offering synchronous and asynchronous online classes.

Evidence to support an advantage of in-person learning over online learning has not been widely substantiated (Xiangming et al. 2022). Li and Lalani (2020) found that an average of 25%–60% of students retained more material learned online, compared with only 8%–10% who retained more in a traditional classroom. This finding may be because students require 40%–60% less time to learn virtually at their own pace (Michigan 2020). Giving students the option to learn at their own pace affords them an opportunity to slow down, revisit, and review work or to move ahead according to their abilities and needs.

Challenges for Students

Students in virtual classrooms may feel emotionally distant or cut off from others. Babu and Koduru (2022) surveyed undergraduate students attending virtual classes to learn their opinions on developing emotional intelligence skills while learning online. Although Babu and Koduru's study was limited in scope and did not encompass all students, their results offer several lessons.

They discovered that a majority of the undergraduates surveyed thought that although virtual learning was conducive to sharing and imparting knowledge, it did little to improve their emotional intelligence skills. Most of the students reported a lack of attention, interaction, and recognition from their teachers, and even though they approved of virtual education, there was a lack of relationship building. Most students felt isolated and did not believe they could improve their emotional intelligence skills in a virtual setting.

Unfortunately, this experience is not unusual; online students often report feeling disconnected and emotionally distanced from their learning experience (Webber 2020). Teachers need to become aware of these concerns and find ways to interact and personalize online learning to maintain student engagement.

Challenges for Teachers

In addition to raising challenges with student engagement, the pandemic highlighted teachers' uneasiness in a setting different from the conventional brick-

and-mortar classroom. Teachers who had spent years teaching in physical class-rooms often lacked experience teaching virtually (Brooks and Pomerantz 2017). Many teachers had to reinvent themselves to teach remotely. Even if school districts offered remote professional training, teachers had to familiarize themselves with remote-learning platforms to put new skills into practice.

For some teachers, a lack of self-confidence or competence in teaching online may have come from their having little interest in working with technology, including troubleshooting technical problems. It was not uncommon for technical difficulties to disrupt virtual classroom lessons, which made it even harder for teachers to establish and maintain a connection with their students. Not surprisingly, many teachers felt isolated and experienced a fight-or-flight response when attempting to connect with their students online (Landis 2021).

The Need for Emotional Intelligence in Learning

Even though skills for developing emotional intelligence were introduced to many schools before COVID-19, EI became a vital factor in helping students cope during the pandemic (MacMillan 2020). Emotional intelligence, or EI for short, can be defined as an ability to be aware of and understand, express, and manage one's emotions and to be aware of the emotions in others (Salovey and Mayer 1990). EI is a blend of intelligence, personality, and emotional expression (Petrides and Furnham 2001). An emotionally intelligent person is one who has the capacity to understand the social and emotional states of others and use that information in ways that are wise and compassionate (Nevins 2020).

The idea of multiple intelligences was created by Howard Gardner (1983). Gardner expanded the definition of classical intelligence beyond academic aptitude and scholastic ability to create a theory comprising seven intelligences linked to content. He argued for the educational benefits of establishing connections between teachers and students and of supporting interactions and relationships between peers (Darwish 2021).

In 1990 Salovey and Mayer (1990) coined the term *emotional intelligence.* Their definition of emotional intelligence accounts for how people assess and communicate their feelings, how they manage their own and other people's emotions, and how they use their feelings to organize, inspire, and accomplish their goals.

Five years later, psychologist Daniel Goleman adapted Salovey and Mayer's concept of monitoring and regulating one's emotional intelligence and others' feelings to guide one's ideas and behaviors (Goleman 1995). He created a framework consisting of five emotional and social competencies: self-awareness, self-regulation, motivation, empathy, and social skills (Goleman 1998).

Goleman's work was well received in the working world, changing how some businesses interacted with clients and managers, and it had great impact in education (Editorial Team of Resilient Educator 2013), where it informed the notion of social-emotional learning, or SEL. Within the framework of a school's curriculum, SEL is an instructional approach that fosters social and emotional competencies in students.

Teaching students to develop their emotional intelligence is known to significantly improve classroom environments (Nizielski et al. 2012). Research shows that students who develop strong relationships with their teachers and peers have a positive attitude toward learning and are more comfortable and engaged in school (Agostin and Bain 1997; Darwish 2021). Classrooms where teachers promote EI through the use and regulation of emotions were shown to be the best predictors of students' life satisfaction in relation to behavioral issues (Quintana-Orts et al. 2021).

Students who exhibit anxiety and aggression have difficulty with learning and are more likely to become victims or perpetrators of bullying (Brackett and Rivers 2014b). Emotional intelligence correlates with less bullying and cyberbullying, and it plays an important role in both preventing and intervening in such behavior (Zhang and Chen 2023). Thus, to foster harmonious relationships, teachers must help students alleviate and manage their stress in interpersonal relationships. This focus on EI is critical not only for students' personal development but also for the virtual learning environment.

Emotions Impact Learning

Adults and children experience a range of emotions every day, both in and out of school. Emotions that elicit interest, wonder, passion, creativity, engagement, joy, and curiosity activate the brain and result in a pleasant and motivating learning experience for the individual (Osika et al. 2022).

Student learning is also affected by negative emotions and emotional disorders. Researchers Wortha and coauthors (2019) investigated negative emotions in virtual learning environments. Their study revealed that students with the highest levels of negative emotions showed a significant negative relationship to learning. These detrimental effects were related to lower (self-reported) emotion regulation. Thus, it becomes critical for teachers to both identify and intervene when negative emotions arise in their students.

Emotional reactions should be seen as a vital part of the learning environment since teachers are capable of influencing or directing students' behavior, emotions, academic engagement, and achievement (Lengyel 2023). Oftentimes, emotions can be revealed by facial expressions. During remote learning, teachers may find it difficult to recognize emotions in students because they cannot walk around the classroom and observe students' facial expressions and body language. However, teachers can gain insights on their students' emotions by becoming aware of their temperament (Ekman 1992).

One approach to identifying students' core emotions using mood, facial expressions, and body language is known as *nonviolent communication*. Krneta and Simunic (2021) describe nonviolent communication as a specific way of communicating through speaking, listening, and remaining compassionate and mindful of one's language (use of words). The researchers point out that nonviolent communication enables teachers to consciously enrich the atmosphere in both classroom talk and other communication with students through empathy, tolerance, and compassion. In this way, teachers who teach virtually can develop an awareness of their own language and body language when interacting with students in a remote educational setting.

Goleman's Emotional Intelligence Framework

As stated above, Daniel Goleman (1998) introduced a framework for emotional intelligence composed of five capabilities: self-awareness, self-regulation, motivation, empathy, and social skills. These five capabilities, which are relevant to both students and teachers, work together to improve emotional responses and develop relationships. Goleman's framework for EI along with his work in SEL has been implemented in schools around the world.

1. Understanding Self-Awareness

Self-awareness is key to emotional intelligence. It is the ability to recognize one's own feelings and emotions as they happen. Self-awareness is critical to developing personal insight and to understanding one's self. People who have a strong awareness of their emotions have better tools for guiding their decision-making in life (Goleman 1998).

To foster a virtual self-awareness, it is essential for teachers to have an online presence in a remote setting where students might not be able to see them in person. By recognizing and responding to students in a positive and timely manner, teachers can help prevent students from becoming frustrated or disconnected and instead encourage them to ask questions and offer responses on- or offline. In virtual learning, teachers can teach their students to become more aware of their emotions, to advocate for themselves by asking for help, and to find ways to alleviate the frustration or anxiety that comes with conflict and learning new skills.

2. Understanding Self-Regulation

Goleman (1998) describes self-regulation as the capacity to handle emotions appropriately so that they facilitate, and do not interfere with, the task at hand. Self-regulation allows individuals to remain calm and stay in control before acting.

Maintaining self-control is critical for teachers when addressing conflicts and working with challenging or problematic student behavior in a virtual environment. Self-regulation enables virtual teachers to match their goals with their actions and attitudes and to remain flexible enough to adjust their teaching as needed. It helps to replace negative thoughts with more positive ones.

The lack of self-regulation of emotions is a significant reason why some students drop out of online courses (Lee and Choi 2011). Students with limited self-regulatory skills can face challenges in mastering the effort and organization needed to succeed with virtual learning (Cho and Shen 2013).

Teacher Strategies for Self-Awareness

1	Be mindful of how you feel.
2	Label your emotions.
3	Take responsibility for your feelings.
4	Be aware of any negative thoughts.
5	Predict how specific things can make you feel.
6	Keep a journal on how you managed your emotions.

3. Understanding Motivation

Motivation is an important piece of emotional intelligence that strengthens learning. There are two basic types of drive: intrinsic (internal) and extrinsic (external) motivation. Intrinsic motivation is the desire to do something for one's own satisfaction; because it is internalized and not dependent on outside benefits, it is more enduring than extrinsic motivation. Daniel Pink (2009), however, points out that extrinsic motivators can be effective because, like goal setting, they can focus the mind.

Once virtual teachers determine what motivator works best for a particular student, they can match the student with appropriate opportunities to engage them in learning. For instance, a student who is interested in art may be intrinsically inspired to create a painting that demonstrates what they have learned. In contrast, an extrinsically motivated student may be interested in competing in a math contest. Because competition can increase or decrease motivation in different students, the complexity of motivation presents many challenges for teachers (Epstein and Harackiewicz 1992).

Teacher Strategies for Self-Regulation

1	Practice self-awareness.
2	Meditate.
3	Exercise.
4	Align your goals with values.
5	Be kind to yourself.
6	Keep a journal.
7	Engage in positive self-talk.
8	Seek feedback.
9	Hold yourself accountable.
10	Educate yourself.

Source: Holly Thompson, "What Is Self-Regulation? 10 Skills and Ways to Improve Them," Indeed, September 18, 2021, https://www.indeed.com /career-advice/career-development/self-regulation-skills.

4. Understanding Empathy

Empathy starts with the ability to understand and care about the feelings of others. Goleman (1995) suggests that being able to read nonverbal communication, such as tone of voice, gesture, and facial expression, is critical to understanding the feelings of others. The extent to which we accurately perceive others' feelings and perspectives helps us understand them.

Virtual teachers who model empathy can influence their classroom dynamics by engaging in active listening, validating students' feelings, and encouraging respect for different viewpoints to solve problems. Listening to students and offering help will reassure the students that they are understood and valued.

Individuals who are wired with a built-in bias toward empathy, cooperation, and altruism can develop social intelligence in themselves and nurture it in others (Goleman 2006). Unless teachers monitor their students' emotional intelligence, however, the emotions and reactions of students can go unnoticed, which could hinder their social-emotional development.

Virtual teachers may benefit from professional development that instructs them on how to nurture social intelligence in themselves and in their students. Especially in times of uncertainty and change, recognizing and managing one's emotions can help individuals acquire habits that promote mental well-being and make them more empathetic toward others.

Teacher Strategies for Motivation

1	Show students you care about them.
2	Build on your students' interests.
3	Make learning fun.
4	Understand what motivates your students.
5	Celebrate your students' successes.

5. Understanding Social Skills

An individual's social skills include the capacity to identify and understand their own feelings and responses, including how their feelings impact their experiences in life (Goleman 1995). This capacity is essential for establishing and maintaining satisfying and healthy relationships.

One component of social skills is decision-making ability, which is demonstrated and developed in domains like leadership (Pappas 2015). Decisions and actions are influenced by intuition and emotional responses (Markic 2009). Making wise choices requires an awareness of one's own feelings and the capacity to control them. When making an emotional decision, people should take time to reflect and consider alternative possibilities (Lehrer 2010).

Teacher Strategies for Empathy

1	Listen attentively.
2	Ask questions.
3	Imagine yourself in someone else's shoes.
4	Share who you are.
5	Validate the feelings of others.

A study from Cornell University reported that emotional intelligence helps individuals make wise decisions (Clemons 2022). It found that individuals with higher emotional intelligence were better at recognizing body cues in both themselves and others and could use that information to avoid making unsafe decisions. Conversely, individuals with lower EI often misinterpreted or did not detect subtle body language.

Teachers make many decisions every day, filling various roles such as disciplinarian, curriculum writer, educational instructor, and leader. Identifying what they think and feel when making decisions about their teaching and course content can help teachers gain a sense of control over the experience (Pappas 2015).

Teacher Strategies for Social Skills

1	Consider your choices before making a decision.
2	Keep an open mind.
3	Analyze social cues and reactions.
4	Express gratitude to others.
5	Take responsibility for your mistakes.
6	Be kind to yourself.

Social and Emotional Learning Impacts Academic and Personal Success

Learning improves when students are motivated, interested, and fully engaged. To help students integrate their behavior, thoughts, and emotions in ways that promote academic performance and personal development, teachers can integrate components of emotional intelligence into their curricula and teach the set of skills known as social and emotional learning, or SEL. The Collaborative for Academic, Social, and Emotional Learning (CASEL) organized the SEL skill set into five competencies (the first three of which are part of Goleman's framework): self-awareness, self-management, social awareness, relationship skills, and responsible decision-making (Jones and Doolittle 2017). Throughout this book, lists containing CASEL's SEL skills provide teachers with a tool to direct student learning through open-ended, purposeful, and relevant questions for creating course content.

Social and emotional learning promotes academic performance and personal development (Jones and Doolittle 2017; Quilez-Robres et al. 2023; Vega 2012). In addition, research shows SEL can improve relationships, lessen behavioral problems, encourage positive behaviors, and enhance mental health (Durlak et al. 2011; Greenberg et al. 2017). Teachers who prioritize, model, and intentionally use educational strategies and teaching techniques that target their students' emotional development can help cultivate student learning in an online classroom environment.

TEACHING TIP

Question

My biggest challenge is knowing how my online students are feeling and what they're learning without stressing myself out. What can I do?

Answer

Oftentimes teachers are unsure of how their online students are feeling in the class and outside the class. To help alleviate the uncertainty, teachers can officially check in with students every few weeks. This can be done through simple online surveys that take minutes to complete. The same survey can be used several times so that students know what is coming and so the data can be easily compared. By doing this, teachers can more easily adjust course content to better fit students' ability level and personalize the content for each student.

CHAPTER 2

Connecting Teachers with Students and Parents Online

Logging into the webinar room for the first time with students looking back at me was a surreal experience. I knew how to navigate the online platform and had been in similar webinar rooms socially, but I was not prepared for the feelings I got. I literally felt as if I had never taught before—like I didn't know how to connect to my students and like I didn't know how to create an online classroom environment. It all seemed so new.

—SHEILA Z., classroom and online educator

Fear of Lost Connections

When discussing online learning, teachers often express concern about the potential loss of the teacher-student relationship. This fear of lost connections was exacerbated after the sudden shift from in-person instruction to online instruction in the early days of the COVID-19 pandemic (Pešikan et al. 2021). Many teachers who were used to in-person classroom instruction found themselves having to connect with their students in a different way. Physical proximity and hands-on lessons were taken away, and teachers had to attempt to connect and communicate through a screen. Many teachers were left with a new sense of distance between them and their students, and they were not given the tools they needed to learn how to connect through the online interface (Turner and Brannon 2022).

Making Connections in the Virtual Classroom

As mentioned, research shows that students' academic achievement and social success are greatly impacted by their social-emotional intelligence as well as by their interactions and attachments with their teachers (Krcmar and Karge 2019). Teachers who carefully design and create an individualized online teaching environment may encourage increased student commitment and interest in the topics (Štibi et al. 2021). Additionally, effective communication between student and teacher in a virtual classroom positively impacts student motivation (Yaşlıca 2020). Therefore, the pressure is on for teachers to connect with students and create a welcoming online environment for them (Ekornes 2017). Unfortunately, technology alone cannot ensure that teachers and students engage and connect with one another (Turner and Brannon 2022).

Much of what helps teachers effectively connect with students in the brick-and-mortar classroom can be translated into components that create successful and meaningful connections in the virtual classroom. Social neuroscience reveals that social processing and learning involve internalizing one's own subjective interpretations of the feelings and actions of others (Uddin et al. 2007). According to Immordino-Yang (2008), individuals operate some of the same brain systems when experiencing vicarious feelings and behaviors as when encountering their own reality. It can be inferred that teachers perceive and understand their students' feelings and behaviors in relation to their own beliefs and goals by vicariously experiencing them. Because we make similar affective neuroscientific connections in our bodies and minds to process emotions, either vicarious or real, social neuroscience shows us how to understand others.

Evidence of these links between people can be seen in an online environment as well. Lengyel (2023, 231) found that "students are significantly influenced by social-emotional factors during their learning activities: the teacher-student, student-student relationship, belonging, emotional warmth, and emotional attachment enrich the students' professional intelligence." Therefore, to ensure that these relationships get off to a positive start, it is important for teachers to begin by opening the lines of communication (Pânişoară et al. 2020).

Flow of Communication

Understanding the flow of communication is important for developing emotional intelligence. By establishing appropriate behaviors and modeling contexts and customs, communication skills help people improve their emotional intelligence and promote a positive and productive work environment. Emotional intelligence makes it possible to control emotions and resolve conflicts across the educational team (e.g., teacher to family and family to teacher) (Dâmbean 2021).

Establishing open lines of communication between all parties involved, including students and their parents or guardians (henceforth, parents), is critical for teachers. Depending on the communication system, interactions between teachers and families can be complicated. Many challenges can block effective communication, including cultural, emotional, language, and perceptual barriers (Dâmbean 2021), and by being aware of these obstacles, teachers can circumvent these obstacles where applicable.

Emotional intelligence skills help teachers adapt to specific situations. By using emotional intelligence, they can modify their communication style to fit the receiver's behavior and personality: "Emotional intelligence is not about changing who you are to become someone else, but it is about understanding and adapting so that you can effectively communicate" (Nguyen et al. 2019, 60).

Using Empathy to Connect

When teaching a classroom of students, teachers need to be able to attend to the outward behavior of their students while keeping their own feelings in check. Having empathy encourages teachers to be curious about the reason behind why someone is behaving in a certain way. It allows teachers to focus not on themselves but on what's happening to another individual. The ability to place oneself in another's shoes in order to gain perspective for understanding is a crucial component of information exchange.

A teacher who has empathy is aware of their own emotions and has the capacity to better understand the feelings and needs of others. Boettcher and Conrad

(2010) call for online teachers to develop good practices for guiding the knowledge development of students and for building satisfying learning relationships by paying attention to each student's engagement and progress. Online tools such as announcements, chats, discussion forums, emails, social media apps, and direct messaging can create teachable moments by demonstrating teachers' active listening and helping them understand their students' needs.

Empathy is important in both student-centered and parent-centered communication. Parents and students should be addressed as individuals—by using their names in correspondence, for example—to convey that the student, parent, and teacher are all part of an educational team (Ruedas-Gracia et al. 2022). Personalizing communications demonstrates respect for the individual while recognizing and validating the bond being created. When students don't feel they are recognized, they can feel unappreciated and lose their motivation to learn. Building connections through listening and constructive dialogues, along with using the communication style that works best for both the teacher and the family, will help improve communication between all members of the educational team.

Communicating with Empathy and Trust

Building relationships with students and parents requires teachers to communicate with empathy and trust. This takes time and effort on the part of everyone involved. Teachers and parents who work together as a team can build a relationship that fosters a child's success and mental well-being. Teachers who keep parents well informed about their child's progress and actively listen to their feedback will build a culture of trust.

A successful teacher-student and teacher-parent relationship is based on communicating openly, demonstrating empathy, and building trust through collaboration. By working together and listening to and understanding students' needs, teachers and parents can address any challenges that arise and create the best possible supportive online learning experiences.

Effective communication with open dialogue may improve the chances to create positive and emotional connections online (Duzgun 2022). Teachers and parents must work together to facilitate a positive learning environment that will ensure the student is engaged and happy while learning online (Asih et al. 2022). Teachers can facilitate effective communication and a positive learning environment by addressing the following four areas of communication: making initial connections, establishing classroom climate, identifying modes of communication, and setting expectations.

1. Making Initial Connections

Teachers will need to make connections with both students and their parents. Initial teacher-student connections set the tone for the class and lead to the creation of a class culture that will support the class during their time together. Making connections not only supports students' emotional intelligence but also impacts the teacher-student experience in the virtual classroom. Positive initial interactions between students, as well as between teacher and students, are essential to students' emotional health and success in the virtual classroom (Bradley-Dorsey et al. 2022).

Teachers can keep the initial contact simple, including a brief introduction to let students know how to be in contact with them. During the initial contact with the student's family, teachers might want to ask an exploratory question (e.g., "What are you hoping to learn this year?" or "What are you hoping your child will learn this year?") or have the student or parent fill out a form to be returned during the initial family contact. This will help ensure that the whole family receives any communication from the teacher, mitigating any future confusion that may result from erroneously excluding some families. Early communication helps families know that the teacher is available to address their concerns and answer their questions before a situation develops that warrants a conversation.

2. Establishing the Classroom Climate

Before students even enter the virtual classroom, teachers establish their first contact with their students by communicating with their families. Creating an early relationship with students and their families establishes the teacher as an authority figure and strengthens the connection between student, parent, and teacher. A teacher should always present themselves as an authoritative figure with a respectful and accepting communication style. Then, as a rapport with students and a classroom culture develop, teachers can transition into a more casual or conversational tone. Students often appreciate a conversational tone, as it helps them feel comfortable and connected to the teacher (Conklin and Dikkers 2021). Realizing that the teacher is a human being and has a sense of humor can benefit the teacher-student relationship, particularly after the class culture has been established.

As with parent communication, the initial connection a teacher has with students sets the tone for the course. In a brick-and-mortar classroom, the teacher establishes the social, emotional, and physical aspects of the environment that, in turn, creates the classroom climate. The class climate or culture funnels into the relationships teachers build with individual students. Similarly, the individual connection between teacher and student is one of the most important aspects of the virtual classroom (Frisby and Martin 2010).

As teachers strive to build a trusting relationship with parents, they sometimes convey a relaxed tone, but setting a relaxed tone early in the relationship with parents can lead to problems down the road. This tone may compromise the parent's perception of the teacher as an authority figure or informed individual, potentially detracting from the teacher's credibility (Sull 2020). Teachers will find it easier to navigate disciplinary procedures by having a professional relationship early on based on open communication. They will also find it easier to become more relaxed, rather than become stricter, as time goes on.

The following are some ideas for how to maintain an open dialogue between teachers and families:

- Create video greetings at the beginning of the semester.
- Send semi-frequent emails—in the sweet spot between nothing and overwhelming communication.

- At the beginning of class, engage the students in dialogue by encouraging them to share news or offer brief catch-ups.
- Before each class, allow students to chat and connect with each other, then establish a transition period and ease into class time.
- Connect students to each other and promote social skills while building friendships through student-centric group messages.
- Foster subgroups by segmenting the class into teams based on interests or group projects.
- At the end of each communication, ask students for their concluding thoughts and/or welcome questions.
- At the end of each lesson, build in a few minutes of class time for reflection and sharing.

3. Identifying Modes of Communication

Schools and other educational organizations may have criteria for teachers' mode and style of communication. In that case, teachers should first defer to the criteria set by their school or organization. Within the established criteria, teachers will want to choose a mode of communication that works for them. The more the teacher tailors the method of interaction to fit their preferences, the more effective the communication between the teacher and family members is likely to be.

At the same time, the teacher should keep in mind each family's preferred method of communication. If a teacher's preferred method does not work well when communicating with a parent, the teacher should make adjustments that are comfortable for both teacher and parent.

Possible modes of communication include phone calls, emails, webinar meetings, discussion board postings, faculty blogs, and virtual office hours. It is recommended that teachers include email or messaging as a mode of communication to give students and their parents a retrievable record of all communication about a course (Ko and Rossen 2010). Having a record of communication, including email replies, can also help teachers if an issue arises. Teachers should maintain general records for at least four years, and longer for specific incidents, and refer back to correspondence to better assess a situation.

When choosing a communication method, the teacher should be mindful of their audience so they choose the method that will best work for their situation. Some schools and educational organizations allow for using social media platforms to connect with older students. Instead of relying on one mode of communication, it is recommended that teachers use more than one mode whenever possible to ensure important information and messages are received (Conklin and Dikkers 2021).

The ultimate goal of communication is to bring together the main stakeholders: the student, their parent(s) and the teacher. Working together will foster a unified and collaborative working relationship which will ultimately benefit all parties involved, especially the student. A student's engagement, academic progress, and emotional growth improve when the student is included in their learning plan and given the capacity to personalize their learning (Petrova 2020; Uysal and Elgün 2022).

Many teachers like to send a welcome letter to students and their families before the course begins. In the letter, teachers should share information about the online arrangements before the first class meeting to give students enough time to get acclimated to the system. For example, students will need to know how to set up and test the microphone, where to locate the classroom and recordings, and how to find the webinar session (see box).

Once the initial connection has been established with students and parents, it is important to keep an ongoing flow of communication with the family. The teacher should make every effort to respond in a timely manner when a parent or student initiates communication (Conklin and Dikkers 2021). Maintaining a predictable flow of communication encourages regular parental involvement and establishes a pattern of consistency that families can rely on. To solidify a strong working relationship, teachers need to go beyond the minimum communication criteria set by their educational organization. For instance, if a criterion is one email a month, teachers may send out two emails a month, making sure to commit to only what they are realistically capable of achieving.

Sample Welcome Letter

Dear Gina,

Welcome! I am so excited you will be joining me for "Women in Science" at Athena's Advanced Academy this spring! We are going to have a lot of fun exploring and learning this semester.

Our first webinar will be on Monday, March 25, at 9:00–9:50 a.m. Pacific time.

To get ready for our first webinar, please complete the Welcome Activities located in the virtual classroom. These Welcome Activities will help you get acclimated to the virtual classroom and the webinar room. You can find the Welcome Activities by following these steps:

- Log into our virtual classroom website [link] with your username and password.
- Click on "My Courses."
- Navigate to the "Women in Science" classroom.
- Locate the Welcome Activities listed there, and complete them before our first webinar.

I would also like you to visit our Resource Room [link]. Here you will find information about our virtual classroom, the webinar room, and the academic calendar. You will also find the link to the practice webinar room. Please log into the practice webinar room and test your microphone to be sure that it works for you.

For our first webinar, the webinar room will be open 10 minutes before class. If something happens and you aren't able to make it, please email me at [teacher's email address] to let me know. If you happen to miss a webinar, you will be able to access webinar recordings in the classroom.

Gina, I'm very glad you signed up for my course. If you need help with anything, please email me. I'm looking forward to getting to know you!

Warm regards,

Dr. Monita

Monita Leavitt, PhD
Online Instructor
Athena's Advanced Academy

4. Setting Expectations

Clear and unambiguous guidelines can help ensure understanding and satisfaction in an online course for both teachers and students (Boettcher and Conrad 2010). Because misunderstandings can happen when virtual learning challenges arise—such as confusion about time zones or malfunctioning technical equipment—teachers should clarify how things will operate so everyone is on the same page.

Adopting a strict rather than a relaxed leadership role is helpful when setting official homework policy. Without clear goals, students might not challenge themselves to reach their full potential. If homework is required for an online course, the teacher should review guidelines with both students and parents at the beginning of the school year. It is important to welcome students' questions to clarify what they need to know about successfully completing homework or projects. Some teachers require a signature from both students and parents so there is a record of agreed-upon policy expectations. Misunderstandings can be avoided later on when policies have been communicated upfront.

The way teachers communicate with families begins by setting realistic expectations for the course. Teachers need to set communication criteria that are comfortable for everyone involved. The frequency of communication depends on whether or not the teacher is an independent contractor or works for a school or educational organization. Teachers need to convey the parameters of their accessibility to their families. In addition, if teachers are unable to reply to their e-mail for a certain period, they can set up an out-of-office reply so families will stay informed and will not be concerned if there is a delay in their response.

Teachers might want to include office hours and their availability in the class syllabus. They may offer office hours to help individuals who have questions get started. Office hours afford teachers a chance to listen empathetically to students (Cacciatore 2021). When virtual teachers demonstrate compassion and care for students individually, students are more likely to assume responsibility and become involved in learning.

Expectations and clear boundaries can be shared through both the syllabus and the virtual classroom. In both, teachers can include information about what students can expect to learn as well as what skills they will gain in the class to help them understand the purpose of the work in their future (Sabila et al. 2022).

Trust between Teachers and Students

Students rely on their teachers to resolve online learning issues through effective, creative, and diverse instruction and caring communication. Evidence shows that when teachers fulfill such expectations, students' learning outcomes and well-being improve. When those expectations are not met, students feel burdened, confused, and overwhelmed (Zorkić et al. 2021).

At the same time, teachers' trust in their students affects teacher competence and conduct. Therefore, to create a mutually trusting relationship, teachers and students would benefit from communicating in a way that allows them to learn more about each other's perspectives and develop empathy (Zorkić et al. 2021).

Creating a mutually trusting relationship will help students and teachers to better communicate, especially if something unexpected happens. If an issue occurs, teachers should be mindful of what they say and how they respond to students. Teachers who show empathy for their students might help them become more emotionally intelligent and thus better able to deal with problems. Conklin and Dikkers (2021) found that "students highly valued instructors who reached out via email or announcements, noted an understanding of the situation, and otherwise demonstrated they cared about the students, the situation, and student learning. . . . Based on the data, to create a feeling of trust and acceptance and a community, the instructor must show a high degree of empathy towards students' learning" (142–43).

Sometimes students do not reach out to their teachers or return communication. A student may find it difficult to discuss problems with a teacher if the student lacks communication skills or believes no one will listen to them. Nonetheless, teachers should encourage open communication in the classroom. Encouraging students to openly express their feelings and thinking can promote acceptance and build a trusting relationship with their teacher. A strong and positive teacher-student relationship promotes student success (Mărgăriţoiu 2020). The following are some ways teachers can foster communication with students in an online setting (Mărgăriţoiu 2020; Ministerul Educaţiei Şi Cercetării 2020):

- Whenever possible, assist and encourage students who struggle with online communication.
- Learn about students' prior educational experience, especially as it pertains to challenges with online learning.
- Help students improve their technical skills for working online.
- Learn about the students' interests and assist them in their endeavors whenever possible.
- Be sensitive to the fact that students have different styles of communication.
- Help foster student accountability.
- Promote critical thinking.

Building a Relationship with Parents

Effective communication between teachers and parents creates a positive and supportive learning environment for students (Asih et al. 2022). Unfortunately, miscommunication can lead to hard feelings and negatively impact the relationship between teacher and parent. If a student's parent does not get along with the teacher, the student is more likely to suffer academically and have a negative relationship with the teacher (Farmer 2020; Westerberg et al. 2020). On the other hand, parents who are comfortable with the teacher may promote a positive student-teacher relationship. The teacher-parent relationship extends beyond the student and can greatly impact the teacher as well.

In an online setting, parents are often the teacher's first point of contact since they are usually the ones registering their child for classes. Alternatively, teachers may choose to meet students first or students and parents at the same time.

Regardless of when they first meet, the teacher should foster a healthy working relationship with the parents, who are ultimately responsible for their child. Whether the student receives instruction from the teacher just once a week for a month or for many hours each week during the academic year, building a working relationship with parents will help to build trust and connection with both parents and students.

Negative relationships with parents have been found to be a strong predictor of teacher stress (Ekornes 2017), and thus working to foster a positive relationship with parents may help mitigate teacher stress. Additionally, when a parent has a good rapport with the teacher and their child does not, the parent may be able to help the child build a positive working connection with the teacher. This kind of positive shift supports the student's emotional intelligence.

Students with parents who actively participate in their schooling and who have a positive, respectful relationship with their teacher typically exhibit higher motivation and greater achievement while being better adjusted socially, behaviorally, and emotionally (Fan and Chen 2001; Powell et al. 2010). This trend is seen at all levels, from the lower grades through high school, where students whose parents trusted their teachers earned more credits and achieved higher grade point averages than students for whom this was not the case (Adams and Christenson 2000). Additionally, students whose parents trusted their teachers demonstrated a higher interest in their school subjects (Lerkkanen and Pakarinen 2021).

The relationship between each stakeholder (student, parent, and teacher) impacts the others. Therefore, fostering open and effective communication between student, parent, and teacher will not only support the student but also lower stress levels in all three groups (Westerberg et al. 2020).

As schools move their classes online, there is an increased need for supportive and engaging modes of both synchronous, real-time communication and asynchronous communication with a delayed response (Villarreal-Davis et al. 2021). Because online teachers may not have the option of participating in a face-to-face conference with families, alternative ways of communicating are required to both inform and engage parents in their child's education.

Before the First Webinar

Following the initial communication between teacher and student, the teacher should provide the rules of conduct for behavior and can then give students time to introduce themselves to the class. When opening up communication for student introductions, teachers should include themselves in the introductions. For example, if the teacher creates a virtual forum with writing prompts where students are asked to introduce themselves, the teacher should answer the same questions to provide an example and to foster the class culture.

Oftentimes teachers wait until the first webinar session to make introductions or begin icebreaker activities, yet there can be advantages to implementing getting-to-know-you activities before the first webinar. Icebreakers tend to favor students who are extroverted, but they can be difficult for students who are not comfortable being the center of attention or who are neurodivergent. Implementing these activities before the first webinar in an asynchronous manner allows shy or neurodivergent students to ease their way into the situation or class.

The activities the teacher chooses to help students connect will be based on their school's online platform. One simple yet effective icebreaker is a forum in the virtual classroom where the teacher asks simple questions and invites students to respond. The teacher can include an introduction answering the same questions from their own perspective. Since storytelling helps build connections, the teacher might also include age-appropriate and situation-appropriate stories about themselves (Kemp et al. 2021)—tales about their favorite things, their pets, trips they've taken, or their experiences with the class topic.

Questions for the class could include the following:

- *What would you like to be called?* Some students may want to be called by a name that differs from the name on their profile.
- *How do you pronounce your name?* Mispronouncing a student's name can be harmful to them or cause them emotional pain (Bratsis 2017). Therefore, every effort should be taken to pronounce their name correctly.

- *What are your preferred pronouns?* Asking students how they want to be addressed, including asking their pronouns, can help them feel comfortable and like they belong (Ruedas-Gracia et al. 2022).

- *Where do you live?* This question is appropriate for students living in different communities or countries, as it allows students to learn more about where their classmates are located. Teachers should be sure to remind students not to give exact locations.

- *What do you like about where you live? What would you recommend someone do when they visit your city or town?* Asking students to share details about their town helps them take on an expert role.

- *Include questions to connect them with the particular class.* For example, in a literature class ask about their favorite book; in a history class ask who their favorite historical character is and why.

- *Include an activity or questions that have an element of fun.* For example, in a literature class, ask students to create a comic with their favorite characters; in a history class, ask historical questions whose answers will come together to solve a puzzle (Sull 2020).

After writing their initial responses, the teacher may request that students reply to others' posts, giving them a sense of control by making this request optional (Milman 2020).

An internet search may yield a number of online icebreaker activities, and the icebreakers teachers choose should be selected with the emotional intelligence of students in mind. Although teachers cannot please every student all the time, they can take the feelings of as many students as possible into consideration.

Teachers should avoid icebreaker activities where students may feel they have been put on the spot. One frequently used icebreaker pairs up students or instructs them to find someone new to chat with. The pair is instructed to ask questions to learn about their partner, remember details about their partner's life, and then introduce their partner to the group. In an online situation, these activities can be done either asynchronously in the virtual classroom or with the assistance of breakout rooms in a webinar. This icebreaker aims to help students connect with an individual and with the group, but it may put undue pressure on students who already feel uncomfortable, including those who are introverted, shy, or neurodivergent. Instead of immediately introducing activities like this, where students may feel pressured to participate, teachers should save them for later, when the class has had a chance to know each other better and when this kind of interaction will encourage students to develop deeper and more meaningful relationships.

Icebreaker activities should be designed to help empower students and give them the opportunity to feel comfortable with one another at the beginning of the course or school year. They can be done over time so students do not feel pressured to participate. Most of these activities can be modified so teachers can implement or add to them throughout the course:

- *Photo collage.* Each student finds a photo on the internet that represents them or something they enjoy. Each one explains (either live or asynchronously) why the photo was chosen. The photos can be gathered together to form a collage in a computer program.
- *Location map.* On a map of the globe, students put a mark on the general spot where they live. If all of the students are from a particular country, a map of the country can be used instead.
- *Short list prompts.* Students are given a prompt to write a short list. For example, "If you were going to go to live in space and could only take five things, what would you take?" The teacher can then compile the lists and note the similarities and differences.
- This *or* that *questions.* Teachers display a simple poll presenting "this" or "that" where students choose their preference. After revealing the response, the class can then discuss the outcome of the poll.
- *Things we share.* The class creates lists of "things we share" to see what they have in common. Teachers can ask questions like "What is your favorite holiday?" or "What do you collect?"

During the First Webinar

The high level of communication created before the start of the course should continue into the virtual classroom and be reflective of the class culture. In the first webinar, the teacher can begin with a brief reintroduction and remind students what they already know about each other. The teacher can then explain how to carry out other getting-to-know-you activities and/or a similar learning-based activity that students can complete together as part of the first webinar.

Students can be anxious when arriving in a class for the first time, even if they have already learned a little about their teacher or classmates. To help ease their stress and anxiety, teachers can implement mindfulness activities that encourage self-regulation so students can identify their feelings and focus on responding rather than reacting. Writing a gratitude list, visualizing what it would be like to accomplish a goal, listening to music, and recording impressions in a notebook are a few examples of mindfulness exercises that can be adapted for any age level. By practicing mindfulness themselves, teachers become better at managing their own emotions and behavior, thereby modeling this emotion and behavior management for their students.

Teachers should avoid calling on students individually unless they have raised their virtual hand. They should invite students to participate, rather than forcing them to participate, to allow students to actively take part in the group at their own pace.

After a brief reintroduction of themselves, teachers may want to review any "housekeeping" (rules and regulations) items they feel are necessary. The tone teachers set through the introductions helps to create the desired class culture. Teachers who hold expectations that the students will live up to the rules improve the likelihood of a successful class cohesiveness (Boykin and Noguera 2011).

Teachers should give students opportunities to start forming a group dynamic as soon as the class starts. This can be done through learning activities that offer students the opportunity to volunteer. Teachers should provide students with positive feedback on the behavior that supports the class culture

(Ruedas-Gracia et al. 2022; Sabila et al. 2022). It is important that teachers have a positive attitude and focus on the class as if it were already a cohesive group.

To engage students, the teacher needs to be engaged (Boykin and Noguera 2011). If the webinar camera is turned on, the teacher should be appropriately dressed and visually engaging. Without video, the teacher must rely more heavily on tone of voice. A welcoming, excited tone helps draw students in and keep them focused on the classroom discussion. This same enthusiasm should be used outside of the webinar.

Webinar Live Chat

Some studies report that, among undergraduate and postgraduate students, the inclusion of video feeds in the learning environment builds community among participants as well as between teacher and student (Sederevičiūtė-Pačiauskienė et al. 2022). In a K–12 setting, however, the effects of video feeds on students, including those with neurodivergent tendencies, have not yet been similarly investigated. For organizations that do not include video feeds in their webinars, feedback or instructions delivered via teacher-recorded video may help connect students with teachers, making students feel as if they are with their teacher and that their course is personalized (Conklin and Dikkers 2021).

A shift from listening to participating occurs when students use the chat box to respond to what is occurring in the webinar in real time (Sederevičiūtė-Pačiauskienė et al. 2022). Courses in which webinars have active chat participation facilitate faster communication and lead to a more cohesive classroom community (Li et al. 2021). To highlight the webinar chat, and to help students become actively engaged without compromising their safety, privacy, or personal comfort, teachers should read and respond to the chat in real time, or as close to real time as possible.

After creating a foundation of effective communication, teachers and students can begin to forge a positive working relationship. Once the class is underway, teachers can use other strategies to strengthen the connections between themselves and their students as well as between students and their classmates.

Bringing Emotional Intelligence to Webinars

WHEN	OBJECTIVE *I will increase students'* *social-emotional skills by . . .*	HOW AM I DOING?	HOW CAN I IMPROVE?

1. Before
the first
webinar
	■ Engaging in initial
	  communication
	■ Implementing
	  icebreaker activities
	■ Improving mindfulness		

2. During
the first
webinar
	■ Making introductions
	■ Presenting choices
	■ Reviewing rules and
	  guidelines
	■ Developing group
	  dynamics		

3. In the
webinar
live chat
	■ Building community to
	  foster relationships
	■ Encouraging students to
	  shift from listener to
	  active participant		

It is important that teachers clarify their ideas by setting an academic goal before the first webinar to focus their efforts. As they revisit this goal during the webinar, teachers can reflect on how they are using emotional intelligence strategies in their teaching practice. The intentional integration of EI in goal setting may increase the likelihood that students will improve their social and emotional skills.

School Relationships Impact Learning

Frisby and Martin (2010) studied how relationships between students and teachers as well as between students and students affect student learning. They found that "perceived instructor rapport was the only variable that consistently emerged as a significant predictor of each type of learning and participation (in students)" (157–58). Student-student relationships did not necessarily help students academically but did promote classroom participation. Therefore, creating a positive, supportive classroom culture and environment can be critical.

A classroom culture focused on learning reflects the paramount importance of the work accomplished by both students and teachers (Bell et al. 2018). This type of culture suggests that high expectations exist for students to learn and grow individually and as a group. The classroom culture should reflect a sense that teachers and students take pride in their work and want to communicate with each other. This culture, which permeates every part of the class, in turn establishes the class's tone.

Ongoing Communication and Trust

Abundant evidence shows that to ensure student success, teachers must effectively connect with their students. Sutherland and coauthors (2019) argue that consistent and frequent communication between teachers and students is critical for an effective teacher-student relationship. Effective communication with the students' teacher and classmates was found to be the best way to keep them engaged with the class and the class material during the pandemic (Santi et al. 2022).

Accordingly, it is important for teachers to foster an open dialogue between themselves and their students, using two-way communication to support an effective virtual classroom (Santi et al. 2022). According to Frisby and Martin (2010), a successful teacher "creates an environment where students feel free to interact, providing a comfortable space that enhances student-student relationships and instructor-student relationships" (157).

It is best to provide students with multiple ways to communicate so they can receive and share information in a way that works best for them (Conklin and Dikkers 2021). For instance, a teacher can both email information to the student and write it within the learning management system. Giving students communication options allows them to pick how they feel most comfortable engaging.

This in turn can help teachers leverage students' emotional intelligence, which can help increase effective communication and reduce stress (Nguyen et al. 2019).

While communicating with students using a variety of techniques and at their comfort level, teachers should be aware that certain learning environments permit the use of particular modes of communication while others do not. While social media platforms may be inappropriate for younger students, for example, they may be acceptable for older students. Still, the platform used must be appropriate for the educational situation. Which social media platform is chosen for communication will depend on students' ages, ability levels, access to technology as wel as the teacher's comfort level and access.

Building trust through effective communication is vital for a healthy virtual classroom culture that supports emotional intelligence (Pešikan et al. 2021). Teachers inspire trust in students by supporting them through the learning process, especially when students struggle. Students inspire trust in a teacher by speaking openly and honestly about their struggles. Both students and teachers can inspire trust in each other through open communication and keeping their word. This trust provides a basis for collaboration and cooperation that can benefit both students and teachers and promote the confidence students need in their academic endeavors (Platz 2021).

TEACHING TIPS

Question

How can I help my students become more self-aware and better connected with their emotions?

Answer

Journaling is a great tool for students to identify, process, and cope with their emotions. One approach is a reaction journal, where students record their reactions—that is, their ideas and feelings—through words, drawings, or both, along with the academic topic they are recording. Keeping a reaction journal encourages students to build self-awareness while making connections to themselves, the text, or their world. When a child shares their journal, teachers and parents can gain a deeper understanding of the child's feelings and perceptions.

Question

What can I do to connect with students I see only once a week?

Answer

When a student shares information about their life, the teacher can write it down in a class list to refer to at a later time. For example, if a student shares that they are going to be participating in an event, the teacher can follow up in their next meeting by asking the student how it went. This kind of follow-up allows the teacher to connect with the student on a deeper level.

CHAPTER 3

Fostering a Supportive Virtual Classroom

A positive learning environment is one where everyone can thrive. All
stakeholders need to feel seen, supported, safe, and celebrated!
—FRAN KENTON, founder of Autonome

Active Learning

Through effective communication with students and families, teachers can foster supportive virtual classrooms that engage students as active learners as well
as support their academic and emotional success. Active learning refers to any
instructional method that engages students in the learning process. It extends
beyond listening and passive note-taking to promote skill development and
higher-order thinking through activities such as metacognition—that is, thinking about thinking. Active learning can be an important part of helping learners
connect course activities to what they are learning (Brame 2016). Chickering
and Gamson (1987) argue that students must go beyond listening to become actively involved in instructional activities that involve doing and thinking and engage in higher-order thinking tasks such as analysis, synthesis, and evaluation.

Successful Online Teaching

"One of the main goals of education is to empower people to be self-directed,
lifelong learners who can continue developing themselves as whole persons" (Lee

and Branch 2022, 304). To succeed at teaching online, teachers must apply the knowledge and abilities they have gained to the virtual classroom so they become good role models for students (Štibi et al. 2021). Whether the virtual classroom is part of a formal or casual institution or organization, the virtual classroom is an extension of the teacher and speaks volumes about them.

Teachers should engage in self-reflection and explore their willingness to experiment with alternative approaches to instruction (Bonwell and Eison 1991). They should modify traditional classroom lectures to incorporate active learning (Penner 1984). Lectures in which teachers pause to check for understanding are more supportive of student engagement than traditional lectures (Ruhl et al. 1987). Additional teaching strategies to promote active learning include cooperative learning, debates, drama, role-playing, simulation, and peer teaching (Bonwell and Eison 1991).

The Goal of a Virtual Classroom

The goal of a positive virtual classroom is to create a warm and inviting atmosphere in which students can develop their skills and feel safe to take intellectual risks. Every student brings their own uniqueness to the virtual class. Some students enter the virtual class ready to participate, while others need encouragement and guidance. The challenges students face in the virtual class may be connected to various factors, such as problems with the online platform, difficulties connected to student personalities, or struggles with learning in general. To help students meet these challenges, teachers should work to create cohesiveness—a spirit of open communication and positive relationships among students and between students and teacher—through the classroom culture.

The suggestions offered here and elsewhere should not be implemented all at one time. Teachers should implement ideas slowly, beginning by doing a few things well and setting and meeting moderate goals before venturing to other goals (Tomlinson 1999).

What Is a Virtual Classroom?

The virtual classroom includes a classroom component and a webinar room. For the purposes of this work, *webinar* refers to the live element of the course, where a teacher meets with students in real time. *Virtual classroom* refers to the asynchronous portion of the course that includes the resources and assignments students access and work on independently. Teachers can create the virtual classroom before the class starts and students arrive. They must remain vigilant in checking to see that all links are working and that information is updated throughout the course.

A virtual classroom can be as simple as a series of emailed handouts or as formal as an actual virtual classroom located on a learning management system (LMS). An LMS is a virtual platform where teachers upload information and assignments for students. Students log into the LMS to view the work the teacher has assigned or suggested. Students can complete work in the LMS synchronously, at the same time as everyone else, or asynchronously, whenever the task fits into their schedule. No matter which mode they pursue, teachers should be mindful of how information for asynchronous learning is delivered.

The information presented in the virtual classroom should convey a tone that reflects the classroom culture. The space should be organized to provide families with clear information and instructions, including due dates where applicable. Students value online spaces that include clear information that is organized logically. Creating an organized virtual space that includes clear information on the onset can help eliminate confusion and help start the course on a positive note (Conklin and Dikkers 2021).

Consistency of tone is key because it adds continuity and familiarity (Boykin and Noguera 2011). A predictable classroom environment is one where students understand what is expected of them and know how to navigate within the classroom parameters (Prior 2014). It gives students the stable environment they need to navigate feelings that arise, improve their relationships with classmates, and resolve any conflicts (Pozo Rosado et al. 2022). Knowing expectations and understanding how to navigate within the classroom parameters promotes self-regulation. Cho and Shen (2013) find it encourages students to succeed in online courses.

The virtual classroom and webinar room should set a tone of acceptance. Welcoming a student doesn't end with a welcome letter. As the course progresses, students should feel a sense of belonging. Every opportunity for conversation is an opportunity to help students feel welcomed. Encouraging students to log in 10 minutes before each webinar for informal conversation can foster a stronger teacher-student relationship. When the webinar room is set up as an open and welcoming space, students can engage positively with their teacher and classmates.

Active Listening

One way for teachers to help online learners develop their emotional intelligence in class is by encouraging active listening. Goleman (1995) identifies signs of active listening as facing each other, making eye contact, and sending silent cues that let a speaker know they are being heard. Although these kinds of body and nonverbal signals are basic active listening skills, they are more difficult to discern in a virtual classroom than in a brick-and-mortar classroom.

There are other skills, however, that can be used to engage in active listening. One such skill is paraphrasing (Wu 2020), which involves mirroring someone else's words to assure them they have been heard. Fortunately, this skill can readily be used in online discussions to demonstrate active listening.

Personalizing Learning for Students

Definitions of personalized learning have multiplied as it has become more widely implemented. Here, personalized learning refers to a broad range of approaches and strategies in which teachers promote better learning by meeting students' needs, interests, and goals.

By learning about their students and building relationships with them, teachers can better help students engage with the material. Getting to know their students before class begins can help teachers personalize the virtual classroom. After their initial correspondence, teachers can ask students to share their favorite animals, movies, or songs, or they can ask questions specific to the course. For instance, a literature teacher could ask students about favorite their books or stories. Then the teacher can use the book titles, book covers, or information about the books in class discussions and presentations. It can be useful for teachers to revisit these questions throughout the course to gauge how students are developing and how their interests may be changing. This will also show students that teachers care about them. The process of personalizing the virtual classroom should be repeated for every new student. This kind of relationship building takes time and cannot be rushed (Pressley et al. 2020).

Teachers should ensure that any personalization added to the virtual classroom can be sustained into the future. For example, when meeting in a webinar, teachers may personalize one specific slide in their weekly presentations instead of multiple slides. In this way, teachers can more easily keep track of which slides need to be updated to personalize a course from year to year.

Personalized learning positions students at the center of instruction and empowers them by offering them greater control over their learning experience. There are many ways teachers can provide students with choices and control—for example, by allowing them to set the ways they want to solve a problem, by giving students the freedom to demonstrate knowledge, and by introducing gamified learning to their environment (Raouna 2021).

Because personalized learning relies upon student input, it can inform a focus on the students' characteristics and learning outcomes (Walkington and Bernacki 2020). Walkington and Bernacki (2020) suggest the future of personalized learning

> lies in researcher-practitioner partnerships that embrace learning
> theory, value the practice-based knowledge of teachers and leaders,
> identify and understand the unique affordances of different learning
> contexts, engage in collaborative design-based research, and employ

rich observation of classroom interactions. These are key to well-informed PL [personalized learning] that allows for deep, meaningful connections to be made to fine-grained learner characteristics and that enables students to take ownership of their learning. (249)

Forging Relationships

Teacher-student relationships matter (Cacciatore 2021). Although initial interpersonal connections can and should be made before the class begins, teachers must build on these connections with students during the class itself. Pressley et al. (2020) discovered that "rather than looking to build relationships at non-academic times, the highly effective teachers developed relationships with students throughout the day and school year. The purpose of these relationships was not only to support learning within the classroom, but also help students develop as people beyond the classroom" (620).

In an interview, counselor and teacher Megan Marcus pointed out that, although it can be challenging, effective teachers can form authentic, caring relationships with their students. In a post-pandemic world in which many teachers engage remotely with students, building strong relationships may feel impossible, but teachers can acquire the skills necessary to create them. Just one caring relationship, Marcus explained, can help change the brain's development, heal trauma, and promote learning for a student (Cacciatore 2021).

Building strong and trusting student-teacher relationships is also critical to addressing stress in students. A strong relationship between teacher and student is impactful when it expresses caring, promotes growth, provides support, shares power, and expands possibilities. Teachers should foster these actions through an equity lens that supports positive racial, cultural, and ethnic identity development in students. The more students experience strong teacher relationships, the stronger their engagement, sense of belonging, and learning in school (EdTrust 2021).

Helping Students Develop Self-Regulation Skills

SELF-AWARENESS	SELF-MANAGEMENT	SOCIAL AWARENESS	RELATIONSHIP SKILLS	RESPONSIBLE DECISION-MAKING
How might I help students learn to identify and label their emotions?	How might I encourage and support students to keep disruptive emotions and impulses in check?	How might I facilitate the class so students feel they are cared for and belong?	How might I encourage active listening skills in my students?	How might I help students make constructive choices in how they participate in class and respond to others?

Developing Self-Regulation Skills

Highly effective teachers can help students develop self-regulation skills—those elements of emotional intelligence that monitor and manage thoughts and behavior when responding to a situation. The development of a student's self-regulation skills is important for the classroom culture and for the unfolding of the teacher-student relationship. To help students develop these skills, teachers can reflect upon the questions shown in the table when developing course content and facilitating online webinars.

In practice, teachers can model various approaches to help children develop self-regulation skills. These include engaging in problem-solving, demonstrating time management, and implementing stress management practices. These techniques can help children reset their minds to stay motivated and nurture a positive attitude (Thompson 2021).

Course Structure

Both the cognitive and the motivational quality of instruction in the classroom are important for students' emotions because they influence learning. Cognitive quality refers to structure, clear instruction, and moderately challenging tasks that can promote greater student understanding and increased self-confidence in learning. Motivational quality involves meaningful tasks that catch and hold students' attention and interest and thus reduce boredom (Pekrun 2014). Both qualities can promote enjoyment, because students who are actively engaged and interested often find learning enjoyable.

The way content is presented to students impacts their learning, so for online education to be effective, teachers must make sure their course is interactive, interesting, and motivating (Santi et al. 2022). Although factors such as teacher presence and the availability of technology are important, learning is improved when content is delivered effectively (Kumar et al. 2023).

The structure of a virtual classroom should have continuity, variety, and a consistent tone to capture the students' attention and add interest. In this way, virtual content is similar to a brick-and-mortar classroom—the structure of the walls and furniture stay consistent, but teachers can embellish them to add personality and character. Just as teachers in a physical classroom might add or change items, such as bulletin boards and learning centers, teachers can modify content in the virtual classroom.

Photos, phrases, color, and font can all be changed to add variety to pique student interest and set the tone for a webinar. If a teacher notices students are not paying attention to instructions, for example, they can vary the color and font of their text or add animated slide transitions to catch students' attention when instructions are particularly important.

When creating content, teachers should make sure the information is inclusive and culturally sensitive so all students feel welcome. Teachers should be mindful of inclusivity in the photos, words, and examples they use in their virtual classrooms and in their online webinars. They should also make certain their students are represented in culturally responsive ways in class and that their classes are student-centered, shifting the focus of instruction from teacher to student to give learners a voice in what they are learning (Peng et al. 2023). Creating an inclusive and welcoming classroom culture may help students view others in a positive light and reduce any bias they may feel (Yazıcıoğlu and Aktepe 2022).

When designing and presenting material to students, teachers must be cognizant of the level at which a student is functioning. Material should not be so hard that it unduly challenges and frustrates a child, nor should it be so easy that they lose interest and motivation to learn. This concept is illustrated in Lev Vygotsky's principle of the zone of proximal development, which theorizes that not adhering to this zone impedes cognitive development (Vygotsky 1978).

Teachers should also be mindful of integrating the elements of students' SEL when they are designing their courses. The table provides essential questions teachers can ask themselves in order to include SEL in their curriculum.

Designing and Presenting Material in an Online Classroom

SELF-AWARENESS	SELF-MANAGEMENT	SOCIAL AWARENESS	RELATIONSHIP SKILLS	RESPONSIBLE DECISION-MAKING
How might I personalize the course material and my teaching?	How might I motivate students when they are learning new material?	How might I make connections so students can build on common interests and develop relationships with their classmates?	How might I develop a trusting relationship with my students?	How might I encourage students to make constructive choices when developing their interests?

Webinar Environment

To ensure their live webinars are engaging, teachers should use the technology available to them (Kumar et al. 2023). For content that stays consistent from year to year, webinar presentations, or prerecorded video lessons, can easily be prepared ahead of time. Prerecorded lessons should not include any information that will be dated.

The teacher's approach to the lesson will depend on their method of delivery. One important consideration is whether webcams are used in synchronous webinars. The use of webcams in an online setting is the subject of some debate. Webinar styles vary widely from educational organization to educational organization. Some organizations and schools require live webcams for teachers and students in synchronous webinars. Other organizations require live webcams for teachers and live webcams for students if desired, live webcams for teachers only, or live webcams for those who desire them, or they require that webcams be turned off. If webcams for students are optional, students should not be pressured to turn their cameras on since they may feel undue stress and the use of webcams may raise privacy concerns (Händel et al. 2022; Rajab and Soheib 2021).

Teachers who decide to use a live webcam in their synchronous webinars should take account of their student population. Consideration should be given to long-term participant safety, participant anonymity, and teacher liability (Rajab and Soheib 2021). Teachers should think about factors such as student ages, learning differences, and socioeconomic levels. For example, if students are placed in the class by level instead of age, they may feel uncomfortable seeing much younger or much older students in the class and may be unwilling to participate fully.

Webinars with Webcams

If the webcam is turned on, teachers need to ensure the scene captured on camera supports a welcoming atmosphere. The items they choose to include in the physical background should reflect the ages and ability levels of their students. If the teacher is teaching younger students, they may want to include items that can often be found in brick-and-mortar classrooms such as colorful posters, stuffed animals, and books. Teachers can also include set dressing that relates to what they know about their students (e.g., a virtual background of a solar system). Of course, teachers can add to or change their background as time goes on to update their information and personalize learning for students.

Virtual backgrounds can also add variation. Some organizations insist that teachers use specific virtual backgrounds, while others allow teachers to choose their own. Although some webinar platforms provide access only to licensed virtual backgrounds, teachers may have the option to upload their own virtual background. Selecting virtual backdrops in advance that complement the session's theme and tone can be useful.

Students are often interested in their teachers' lives, and by adding personal touches to their webinar background, teachers can foster students' interest and help students better relate to them. This can lead to positive student-teacher relationships, which benefit student achievement (Sutherland et al. 2019).

How teachers present themselves in the webinar will also impact their relationships with the students as well as help to set the class culture. A teacher who arrives to class wearing disheveled clothes with unkempt hair is not going to convey the same message to their students as they would if they arrived with a polished and professional look. Of course, individuality and personal preference must come into play, but the teacher should be aware of the messages they are sending to ensure they are consistent with a welcoming and supportive learning environment.

On video, teachers need to be aware of their facial expressions and body language. It can be more challenging to exhibit appropriate facial expressions and body language when everyone's attention is focused on the screen than it is face to face. In a face-to-face situation, the teacher may walk around the room or be far removed from their students in a lecture hall. It is common for teachers to turn their backs to their students when writing on a board in a brick-and-mortar classroom. Online, however, the camera is inches away from people's faces, and the platform gives little opportunity for teachers to turn their backs. This means that students can observe the teacher's facial expressions and body language at all times.

When webcams are turned on, teachers should look at the camera rather than at the screen, which gives students the perception that the teacher is looking at them. However, teachers should remember to blink their eyes while speaking since people do not normally stare intensely at others during regular face-to-face conversations. Teachers can also use the video feed to scan their students' faces and monitor their body language.

Webinars without Webcams

When live webcams are not present, teachers must rely on verbal engagement and voice inflection to hold their students' attention. If teachers come to the webinar with a bored tone of voice, the students will likely be bored as well. Conversely, teachers who bring excitement and enthusiasm to their voices when they teach are more likely to engage their students (Boykin and Noguera 2011). Teachers can also add pauses, modulate their voice, and ask interesting or probing questions to serve as catalysts for engagement.

If the energy of the class shifts negatively after a student speaks, it is up to the teacher to bring the excitement back to the webinar room to re-engage students and encourage participation. This can be done in a variety of ways. Teachers may model offering positive feedback, recap what a student talked about, ask for clarification, or ask the class for a real-life connection.

To help create a visual connection, teachers who teach in webinars that do not include a video component may want to create video recordings outside of the webinar. Teachers might record a video message to students before the first webinar session or create several videos over the course of the class. These videos can be conversational and can provide students with additional feedback on assignments that may require more information. Some teachers choose to provide feedback on assignments primarily through video recordings, which can help students who might be sensitive to feedback feel more supported. Video feedback can help minimize misunderstanding, help students overcome learning and socio-emotional obstacles, and support student engagement (Cavaleri et al. 2019).

Webinars with Chat Only

Occasionally, educational platforms conduct instruction exclusively through the use of text chat. Platforms like this are similar to threaded discussions in the learning management system but instead are written in real time. In cases like this, teachers can maintain student interest by introducing new vocabulary and employing distinctive adjectives, adverbs, and other descriptive terms. Teachers can also experiment with using unusual punctuation (e.g., multiple exclamation points) and by adding emojis where applicable. Emojis are a simple, fun way for students of all ages to share their emotions.

Webinar Content

Teachers frequently create slide shows to convey information about the subject, regardless of whether they use webcams. The teacher's presentation serves as the primary visual aid and a vital source for ensuring student engagement in the webinars, particularly if webcams are not used.

Although information placed on slides can stay relatively consistent from year to year, the teacher may want to update the style of the slides on a regular basis. It is beneficial to review slides to ensure they align with the intended audience and current students. The teacher should view the slide presentation through the eyes of their students to understand how students may perceive the material.

Teachers also need to be mindful of the amount of text they post on each screen. To understand how much to post, teachers should think about the information as though students were reading headlines in a newspaper. A good rule of thumb is to allow enough time for the screen to be read twice. Using bullets or arrows is a great way to list ideas. Teachers can use their notes to explain each idea fully, recognizing that students don't necessarily have to have every bit of information written on the screen.

When reviewing the slides, teachers should look for misspelled words, pixelated photos, antiquated themes, outdated slide structure, poor font readability, and obsolete color choices. Some words or content may no longer be appropriate, or an image may no longer look clear. Until recently, for example, it was common to refer to individuals whose identity is unknown as "he/she," but now the use of "they" is encouraged. Similarly, teachers should watch for other gendered and cultural group terms that are no longer in use. Being attentive to cultural shifts will help support students who belong to these groups, particularly as students are now more attuned to the broader culture than ever before.

Photographs and other visuals used on slides should also be reviewed regularly. Teachers should ensure photos of humans used in the presentations include diverse representation so everyone in the class feels included (Moody and Matthews 2021). Some teachers purposely avoid including images of people in their slides to avoid the need to update photos as fashion trends change.

No matter what photos are used, it is good practice to preview slides in the webinar room before their use. As technology advances, photos that looked crisp and clear one year might look pixelated and fuzzy the next. This can be distracting for students, who are used to crisp images in media they consume. Including large, visually appealing photos can also improve the webinar experience.

Visuals in the webinar room are one of the main engagement tools at teachers' disposal, so they should review the ratio between words and photographs to find a balance that engages students. Slides with a white background with a bulleted list of information are unappealing and limit engagement from students who are new or struggling with reading, whereas slides with movement (e.g., transitions), color, visual appeal, and fewer words are more apt to keep students engaged. Switching slides frequently rather than remaining on the same slide for an extended period can also increase student interest (Warmuth and Caple 2022).

Student Interests

As already discussed, including information about students' interests in class materials and presentations can encourage engagement. As the course progresses, the teacher can add new information about the students and the culture of the group (Pressley et al. 2020). Mentioning a running joke in the class, or reminding students about a humorous moment, can help build camaraderie. Including screenshots of students' work and commenting positively on it in real time can boost students' self-esteem, particularly for students who are struggling with aspects of the material. By including students' information in the class slides, teachers empower the students and help them see themselves in the curriculum.

To preserve a positive, trusting relationship with students, however, it is vital not to share students' personal information or information they have shared in confidence. The material teachers share should be information that students have previously shared with the group, information for which student and parents have granted express permission, and information that elevates rather than belittles the student.

Collins and Landrum (2023) postulate that to establish a positive relation-ship with students, teachers must move through three phases: establish, maintain, and restore.

> At the establishment phase, it is important for teachers to make connections with students and establish understanding and trust. Once the relationship is established, it must be maintained by providing regular opportunities for reciprocal communication and positive interactions between the student and the teacher. Finally, in the event of conflict, teachers may need to restore relationships by communicating very intentionally to rebuild connections and trust. (189)

Parental Impact

Emotional learning begins in a child's earliest moments and continues throughout life. How parents treat their child has an emotional impact with lasting consequences. The exchanges between a parent and a child over time influence a child's emotional expectations about relationships and outlooks (Goleman 1995). Thus, both teachers and parents need to be aware of the influence parents have on their child's emotional intelligence.

Over time, parents move from doing everything for their children to giving them more responsibility as they grow and mature, and teachers follow the same trajectory. Teachers provide students with the tools they need to learn at the next level. Although teachers focus on creating a cohesive educational environment with the group as a whole, there is an underlying focus on students as individuals.

Platform for Making Connections

The virtual classroom provides a convenient and flexible platform for making new and meaningful connections, and emotionally intelligent online teaching should use insight and innovation to make the most of this virtual environment (Webber 2020). Starting as a place where teachers welcome students and their families, online courses should bring all stakeholders together so that the class becomes a cohesive group participating together, while still allowing for individualism and autonomy within the group.

In each class, students move from being passive learners to active learners. This begins as the teacher creates a welcoming environment where all students are recognized for their individuality and feel they belong. After welcoming students, the teacher's focus moves to creating a group culture of both cohesiveness and open communication (Händel et al. 2022).

In online environments, establishing psychological safety is critical to enabling students to speak openly and freely (Rawson 2021). Students experience both positive and negative emotions in their virtual environment: they may feel happy and satisfied if they have achieved a goal or accomplished a task, or they may feel sad and frustrated if they give an incorrect answer or face a problem they can't solve. By helping students identify and label their emotions, teachers can help students learn to communicate using their words and feel psychologically safe in their classroom culture.

Establishing Ground Rules for Behavior

After the initial connection, teachers can set the stage for further communication, including how students will interact among themselves. This is an ideal time to establish ground rules for behavior in the virtual classroom and webinar room. Not only do teachers have expectations for conduct in their classrooms, but most virtual schools and educational organizations also have overarching rules and regulations. Instead of rules about hallways and playgrounds, there are rules about chat rooms and webinar etiquette. Providing families with expectations early on helps students and parents feel more prepared to engage with the class structure.

The initial contact between the teacher and the student or family should be a social interaction designed to make everyone feel welcome. Teachers should wait until the second communication to share information about classroom rules and expectations. Providing students and their families with a separate place to review this information separates the greeting from "housekeeping" and helps avoid student trepidation.

How teachers share these expectations and rules depends on the amount of time they have with students. Teachers who meet their students several times a week may have time to discuss the rules. Teachers whose classes meet less often may find it more efficient to go over the rules and expectations asynchronously—through, say, a follow-up email or a link in the virtual classroom—instead of taking class time for this purpose. No matter how the rules are initially conveyed, they should be posted in the virtual classroom for easy reference.

Virtual Classroom Expectations and Rules

As mentioned, teachers will likely want to set rules and expectations that go beyond their school's standards and are specific to their classroom structure. While a school might have a set policy for work submission, for example, the teacher may want to require that students email the teacher when submitting work to the LMS.

Guidelines in the virtual classroom will help shape the class culture. Teachers may set guidelines focused on how students speak to each other, how students conduct themselves in the webinar chat, or what type of material is appropriate for students to discuss and post. Whatever rules and expectations the teacher sets, they need to be mindful of phrasing and tone when writing down those rules. Conveying support and positivity when writing guidelines can be challenging but worthwhile.

Instead of setting expectations and rules directly, some teachers work with students to generate the rules for their virtual classroom, which can produce a more student-centered environment. Teachers can allow students to participate in generating all the rules or add to non-negotiable ones. This approach allows students to take ownership of this process beyond what is usually expected of them, develop self-awareness and emotional intelligence, and work together to mold the class culture (Albert 2020).

Teachers should take time limitations, including the length of the course, into account when creating class rules. Ideally, teachers and students would create virtual classroom rules together in an open discussion during a webinar. If this is not possible, the task can be completed asynchronously. For example, the teacher could create a threaded discussion to allow students to discuss and come up with ideas.

After students and parents have read and agreed upon the virtual classroom rules, teachers can create a questionnaire form for families to fill out, sign, and email to the teacher. By collecting these virtual signatures, teachers have a record to show that parents and students agreed to the rules before or shortly after the beginning of class. The signed agreements will be beneficial if a student does not follow the rules later on in the class. With an agreement in place, teachers can remind the student that they consented to follow the rules. Although this practice may not help in every situation, being able to produce a reminder can help redirect student thinking and behavior.

There may be a time when, for example, a student repeatedly posts nonsense in the chat, drawing attention away from the learning that should be taking place. The teacher can address the situation according to their plan and contact the student and parent after the lesson. In this follow-up correspondence, the teacher can refer to the agreement to follow classroom rules and remind parents of their commitment to the student's education.

Incorporating Curriculum Goals

After establishing an initial class culture, the teacher can incorporate curriculum goals. These goals will be greatly influenced by the online school or educational organization where the teacher works. Objectives and benchmarks are often written into a curriculum, and teachers may have little flexibility within the course if the curriculum is set by the school or overseeing organization. Conversely, if a teacher has autonomy over the curriculum, they may have much more flexibility. No matter what the parameters are, focusing on fostering a supportive virtual classroom environment is imperative to assisting students to become active learners (Pešikan et al. 2021).

Teachers can use the curriculum not only to organize the class content but also to help create the class culture by adding information that pertains directly to the students and what is important to them. Teachers should ensure that the examples they provide are realistic and reflect their students and class culture (Martin and Bolliger 2018).

Supporting the Individual Student

A supportive virtual classroom has a dual purpose: supporting the group and supporting the individual. Unfortunately, it is not uncommon for individual voices to get lost in the group. Although far-reaching legislative measures are often voted into existence to make sure no student is left behind, there are still students who fall through the cracks (Vinovskis 2019). It is important for teachers to recognize all individuals so they receive the attention they need to succeed.

One way for teachers to support students is to encourage their love of learning. Teachers are there to help students discover and develop their voices. Although each class is just one step on their educational path, the connection students have with the teacher could have a profound impact on their future. The table shows essential questions teachers can ask themselves when reflecting upon ways to support individual students in their courses.

Student Work in an Online Course

Student work is key to supporting individual learners. Even though teachers need to abide by their school's requirements regarding curricula and assessments, this should not deter them from supporting their students' emotional intelligence by personalizing student work and assessments. Whether students are achieving above or below grade level, teachers must provide the same support, giving class work and assessments that are appropriate for their level of learning.

Supporting the Individual Student

SELF-AWARENESS	SELF-MANAGEMENT	SOCIAL AWARENESS	RELATIONSHIP SKILLS	RESPONSIBLE DECISION-MAKING
How might I assist each student in sharing their feelings in small groups?	How might I promote individual learning in my classes?	How might I foster leadership in every student?	How might I promote student cooperation and encourage empathy for one another?	How do I encourage each student to interact positively in my classes?

Rolón-Dow (2005) describes the difference between caring *aesthetically*, which entails focusing on the student's work, educational goals, and curriculum, and caring *authentically*, which signifies focusing on the student and their experiences. Although showing aesthetic care is important, caring authentically supports the student, their emotional intelligence, and their educational achievement. For example, if a student misses class, the teacher can reach out and check on them. Instead of focusing on the negative aspect of a missed class or a student's low grade, the teacher could check on how the student is doing and find out what type of support the student needs (Ruecker 2021). Similarly, when assessing a student's work, the teacher needs to provide feedback that shows they care about the student and are invested in the student's progress and achievements.

Because each student is unique and has their own level of excellence, their work should not be compared with any other student's work. No matter how much effort teachers put into avoiding comparisons, students will often compare themselves with each other or with a sibling. When student output is kept private, teachers can tailor their responses to the work accordingly. However, when student work is displayed or shared with the class, extra care should be taken. Teachers should provide similar levels of feedback to all students in the class. Teachers should also encourage students to be supportive listeners and provide their classmates with positive feedback to motivate and encourage learning in online classrooms.

TEACHING TIP

Question

How can I write my class rules to support my students' emotional intelligence?

Answer

Classroom rules should be framed in terms of *dos* rather than *don't*s to keep the focus on the positive. This sets the expectation that students will be *following* guidelines instead of avoiding them. For instance:

- Instead of "Don't be rude," try "Speak kindly to others."
- Instead of "Don't post inappropriate materials," try "Post only appropriate materials."

CHAPTER 4

Engaging Students as Active Online Learners

I find that, when trying to increase student engagement, it is critical to remember that being "engaged" looks different for everyone. Some students might show their engagement by sharing their thoughts in the chat box. Some might feel most comfortable speaking on the microphone and won't participate much in chat. Some will show a deep understanding of the material in the assignments they complete, but you won't hear their voice on the microphone until after you've known them for months and they feel comfortable in the group. Some students make eye contact on a webcam— some will never look directly at the camera. When I am deep in thought, I will look away from my computer screen and stare at something else in the room! Traditional metrics of engagement don't work for everyone—and what's fantastic is that online educators have the freedom to redefine engagement.

—EMMA STEIN, online educator

Engaging Online Students

Whether teaching asynchronously, remotely, or synchronously in a hybrid or brick-and-mortar classroom, teachers want students to be fully involved in learning. For online teachers, however, who cannot walk around the classroom to see their student's faces and observe what they are doing, it is much more challenging to "read the room" in order to accurately assess and encourage student engagement.

Although it may feel daunting at first, virtual teachers can build authentic, caring relationships remotely and learn skills to communicate with students in online as well as in-person classrooms. It is these authentic relationships that can help students reach their personal and academic goals. There are a variety of ways teachers can create opportunities for student engagement in the online classroom, including asking questions, promoting class-wide discussions, and administering class polls. Software platforms that facilitate easy classroom navigation and provide teachers the opportunity to view assignments from their students' point of view can be useful tools to help teachers connect with students. Personalizing communication with students, offering choices, and asking for informal and formal feedback can help teachers build important virtual student relationships. Additionally, holding office hours affords teachers a chance to listen empathetically to students to let them know the teacher cares about them (Cacciatore 2021). When teachers demonstrate compassion and care for students individually, students are more likely to assume responsibility and develop engagement in their learning.

Creating a Welcoming Environment

Students should always be greeted by their name, or preferred nickname, when entering the webinar room. Addressing students by name helps them feel noticed and invites them into the virtual space (Bratsis 2017; Ruedas-Gracia et al. 2022). Depending on the webinar set-up and the teacher's individual preference, the teacher can greet students individually verbally or in the chat area. Modeling this behavior may encourage other students to greet each other as well and can assist in creating a welcoming atmosphere. Time spent with students in the webinar room can help generate a supportive, student-centered environment that engages students and builds both social and emotional awareness.

Engaging through Breakout Rooms

Even simple webinar components, like breakout rooms, can be used to create an engaging atmosphere. When determining which tools to use and when to use them, teachers should consider the class structure and how well students work together, while also keeping in mind their class goals, such as supporting students' emotional intelligence and creating the desired class culture. In general, teachers should not use any online tool until it can be appropriately and effectively used by students in their class.

Many platforms include webinar breakout rooms, allowing teachers to break a class into small groups. Teachers can use breakout rooms to give students opportunities to work in small groups for a project or to provide them with more opportunities to engage in discussion, post their reflections, and share their thoughts (Wilkins et al. 2023). Breakout rooms can be beneficial to students who thrive in smaller groups. Once there, quiet students who prefer smaller groups can express their ideas with a small number of peers before sharing with the entire class (Beeman 2022).

However, breakout rooms may present some drawbacks. Because a single teacher may not be able to be present simultaneously in every breakout room, students may be left without supervision. Students left to their own devices, including those who do not know how to carry on an effective conversation, may not accomplish much in a small group. (Teachers should check their school's rules about students being alone for any length of time without supervision, especially if the webinar room does not have the capability to record the session.) Some students may feel anxious or stressed if they are forced to interact with their classmates in breakout rooms (Wilkins et al. 2023).

To mitigate these issues, the teacher may decide to record the activity in each breakout session. It may be helpful to put additional adults or students in a leadership role within small groups to ensure everyone stays on task. A responsible person, such as a teacher's assistant, could join each breakout room with the students, especially if the students are younger. Ideally, a teacher's assistant would be known to the class and could help engage students in small groups when needed.

Establishing Breakout Rooms

SELF-AWARENESS	SELF-MANAGEMENT	SOCIAL AWARENESS	RELATIONSHIP SKILLS	RESPONSIBLE DECISION-MAKING
How might I develop my awareness of individual students in the breakout room?	How might I help students to build upon their previous breakout room experiences in positive ways?	How might I monitor student activity and collaboration?	How might I support positive student interactions with peers?	How might I discourage negative peer pressure in the breakout room?

When deciding whether to use breakout rooms, teachers should think about the personalities of the students, group dynamics in the class, and class structure. Teachers who meet with their students only weekly may choose not to use breakout rooms because of the limited time spent in webinar rooms. In other cases, keeping in mind the ability levels and emotional intelligence of their students, teachers may decide to wait to use breakout rooms until students are able to work effectively in a group without direct instructional oversight.

Wilkins and coauthors (2023) stress that teachers must do the following before using breakout rooms in their webinar sessions: be aware of the students themselves (e.g., backgrounds, characteristics, learning preferences), understand the students' prior experience with breakout rooms, and make sure the teacher is able to visit each breakout room consistently to help monitor activity and collaboration.

Teachers may find it helpful to consider essential questions that can guide them in establishing breakout rooms that will promote positive social and emotional as well as academic learning experiences for their students, as shown in the table.

Engaging through the Webinar Whiteboard

The webinar room's whiteboard function helps students connect not only with the material but also with other students. Teachers should determine their webinar room's capabilities before providing students with whiteboard permissions. Webinar room capabilities vary from service to service, but they allow users to draw on the whiteboard (or on imported slides) once the function is engaged. Teachers should determine whether whiteboard permissions can be given to individual students or only to the class as a whole.

When they grant permission for use, teachers may select how they want students to use the whiteboard features. Students can use the whiteboard to perform individual, small-group, or whole-class assignments. Before, during, or after the lesson, students can work together on cooperative group drawings, games, or learning activities such as filling in a Venn diagram or creating a mind map on the board. The entire class may also offer feedback by completing a poll or survey on the whiteboard or webinar tool.

In addition to using the whiteboard tools with blank slides, teachers may engage students by using whiteboard tools on presentation slides. Slides can present opportunities for students to participate, such as by posing questions for which students must fill in the blanks. Additionally, teachers can encourage students to create their own slide presentations in connection with a class assignment or because they want to share something they discovered.

Engaging through Webinar Chat

Webinar chat rooms provide students with a platform to share their thoughts, ask questions, and communicate with both the teacher and one another. The chat area benefits students who are quick to add their thoughts and who are not afraid to speak up in class. They can express what they want to share without interrupting the flow of the webinar.

Quiet students can also benefit from the webinar's chat (or similar feature allowing for written responses) by supporting them at their comfort level. Having the option to participate in written form rather than orally helps to bolster their confidence level and allows them to participate in the class with less trepidation (Beeman 2022). Students can formulate their response before sharing it with the group, writing down their thoughts in the chat field and waiting to press enter until they have reviewed what they want to say.

Rules should be established early on about uses of the chat. For example, the teacher might specify that the information students type in the chat before and after class can be social but that the information in the chat area during the lesson should pertain to the lesson itself.

Teachers may find the webinar chat intimidating. It can be challenging to keep students on task if they are active in the webinar chat and not paying attention to the lesson. Many webinar programs allow notifications to be enabled for comments in the chat, which can help teachers catch every message. Teacher's assistants can help by monitoring the chat feed. As teachers find ways to circumvent any behavior issues that may arise in the webinar chat, they will become more comfortable and more confident with using the chat function.

Engaging with Emojis

Emojis and emoticons can be used in the webinar chat to make learning fun. Emojis are symbols from a variety of categories that students can insert in the chat, including hearts and faces, animals and nature, people and travel. Emoticons (short for "emotion icon") use typed characters to express feelings (such as a colon followed by a parenthesis to create a smile or frown).

Webinar chats often include the ability to use emojis, which children, teens, and adults find helpful to express their emotions when communicating online. Although the use of emojis does not always accurately convey emotions, emojis can help teachers and students understand the emotion or tone being conveyed when a student posts in the chat, especially when the student prefers not to use the microphone (Zilka 2021). For example, to learn how students feel about a topic being discussed, a teacher can ask students to place an emoji expressing their feelings in the chat area. Some students may put smiley faces, while others might put confused faces. The teacher can then respond to that feedback and tailor the content to students' understanding.

It is important to note that there are often alternative or inappropriate meanings behind the use of some emojis, so teachers should educate themselves on current meanings.

Engaging through Polls

Some webinar rooms are equipped with the functionality to poll students on yes/no or multiple-choice questions. Teachers may choose to reveal the results of polls to students or keep the results private. Sometimes the class-wide results of the poll can be shown while keeping individual responses confidential.

When using polling, teachers must be mindful of class sensitivities, how students respond to others' opinions, and the class culture the teacher is creating. This does not mean, however, that teachers should avoid every challenging situation. Rather, they should keep the nature of their class in mind so students can learn to navigate challenging situations. For example, in a class of 20 students, 19 of them might vote "yes" while one student votes "no." By modeling how to navigate differences of opinion like this, teachers can nurture students' emotional intelligence. Through modeling, they can demonstrate that individuals who achieve the best results do so through optimism and realism (David 2016).

Sharing Personal Excitement and Difficulties

At some point during the webinar, teachers can interact with their students, and allow students to engage with each other, in a more relaxed manner. Inviting students to share what is going on in their personal lives opens up opportunities for students to engage (Rio Poncela et al. 2021). Taking a few minutes to ask if anyone has anything to share before class begins might help students feel more connected with their classmates and the teacher.

The information students share may be positive or may be challenging. The teacher should be mentally prepared for students to share exciting and uplifting news (e.g., winning a soccer game) or troubling and sad news (e.g., death of a pet). No matter what the news, this sharing gives the teacher and the students' classmates an opportunity to offer support. Teachers should model an attitude of calm receptivity, which puts them in a position to offer empathy (Goleman 1995). This support can occur in the webinar room, in the virtual classroom, or through the modes of communication already established. For example, if a teacher learns information about the family (e.g., having a baby or experiencing a death in the family), they can reach out to the family to connect with them about what is happening at home. Beyond verbal encouragement, a teacher can also take action to support the student. For example, if it appears that the student will need more time for their work because of the home situation, the teacher can offer to extend project deadlines.

For information of any nature, positive or distressing, teachers should make note of it so they can connect with the student about it the next time they meet, further engaging the student.

Classroom Components

To help engage their students while in the virtual classroom, including during the asynchronous portion of the class, teachers should begin by looking for areas of opportunity across the applications they have available, such as the tools in their webinar system and their LMS. For example, if webcams are turned off during the class webinars, the teacher may want to find other ways to connect with their students visually. The teacher may choose to record videos of themselves speaking into the camera to share announcements and information (Brazelton 2020).

The LMS often allows for more individualization than the webinar room, allowing teachers to add colors, pictures, videos, and other components to customize the virtual classroom. As always, teachers will want to keep in mind how their class is structured, how well students work with each other, and the unique nature of each student.

In addition, these classroom components may enable teachers to individualize the learning experience for each student. Students can be provided with a choice of assignments (e.g., term paper, video creation) or given a selection of what medium to use when completing an assignment (e.g., written down, orally shared).

Engaging through Forums and Forum Discussion Threads

Including social interaction in the virtual classroom can help engage students and support their emotional intelligence (McGlynn and Kelly 2020). Some LMS infrastructures allow LMS chat rooms where students can connect in real time, whereas other applications have tools for engaging students asynchronously. To allow for unstructured or freeform discussions through written responses, teachers can set up a dedicated forum for social interaction in a specific spot in the virtual classroom or virtual organization. New social forums can be created and placed with the assignment list each week. Social interaction can also be built into academic assignments, helping students engage with each other on both a personal and an academic level.

Threaded forum discussions—where the teacher posts a prompt in a virtual forum application and students reply to the prompt—create opportunities for students to connect with each other about the academic topic, promoting asynchronous interaction in the virtual classroom. After the teacher posts a forum prompt, students each post a direct reply. From there, teachers should remind students to reply to their classmates' posts. Students should not be asked to reply to every post from their classmates. Instead, teachers should encourage students to reply as many times as makes sense for their ages, grades, and ability levels. Students will be more likely to feel they are heard and to offer insightful and empathic responses if they are required to reply to only a restricted number of other posts.

Cook (2023) found that students engaging in dialogue with other students in online threaded discussions reported greater satisfaction with the course than those who simply responded to the discussion prompt. For teachers, it can be awesome to watch asynchronous online conversations among students unfold.

These conversations can give teachers insights into how their class is interacting and how well they are embracing the class culture.

Threaded discussions can be approached in several ways, some dictated by the school and others set by the teacher. The rules that are established will greatly impact the number of responses and the quality of responses. Certain guidelines for student participation prescribed by the school may generate more responses, but the discussion may not flow. If the choice is left up to the students, participation may be less, but teachers may receive more authentic, conversational responses from students. The amount of student participation will depend on the teacher's involvement, how well the teacher understands the students, the students' motivation, and the students themselves (Cook 2023).

The goal of a discussion thread is to create an educational environment where students participate in the discussions and post responses with real depth. This type of communication can be challenging for a teacher to achieve in a traditional classroom, and even more so in an online classroom, so teachers need to find interesting and unique ways to present discussion prompts as well as responses. Teachers will want to focus on presenting prompts that promote interaction and critical thinking (Cole et al. 2020). They may also want to include examples and images with the discussion prompts to nurture a higher level of critical thinking (Joyner 2012).

Engaging through Personalization of Prompts

Personalizing forum prompts (or any online assignment) may help engage students in the asynchronous portion of the class. Boettcher and Conrad (2010) suggest designing options and choices within learning experiences, assignments, and special projects to support learners with their goals. Personalized options and choices may be based on individual students, groups of students, or the class as a whole. To personalize the prompts, the teacher may adjust the wording of the forum prompt or include another prompt that will engage a particular set of students—for example, including a reference to a recent class discussion in a forum prompt. Such a prompt should be modified every time the class is taught to personalize the course for the current group of students.

Teachers can reference individuals in the prompts, using information the student has shared publicly. They might mention a hobby, movie, or interest—something about a student that is familiar to everyone in the class. Alternatively, they can include student names in their prompts. For example, instead of a prompt that relates to a fictional person, the prompt could name students in the class. Of course, student names should only be used in conjunction with positive prompts (Bratsis 2017; Ruedas-Gracia et al. 2022).

If the teacher personalizes the class with references to individual students, they must remember to include all students throughout the course of the class. Near the beginning of the class, teachers should mention each student at least once, perhaps by referring to groups of students and naming each student. After all students have been mentioned at least once, the teacher can then mention sets of students or individual students as the class advances. This approach means students are not left wondering if the teacher will remember to mention them.

Personalizing a course takes forethought and time, and the amount of personalization the teacher includes will depend greatly on the number of students in the class and the teacher's workload. The teacher may implement it slowly over time or may keep it simple and focus only on personalizing the class forums all at one time by changing the students' names. No matter how the teacher personalizes the forums, they should create a system of checking forums each year so that information from previous years is not shared erroneously with a new class.

Emotional Intelligence through Digital Storytelling

In the virtual classroom, teachers can use digital storytelling to promote student emotional growth. Digital storytelling refers to images, experiences, and narratives shared using technological tools like audio, graphics, and videos (Lisenbee and Ford 2018; Robin 2008). Because of its versatility, digital storytelling can be incorporated into many subjects and courses, including history, literature, and mathematics.

Instead of using digital storytelling only to convey a concept within a particular subject matter, however, teachers can include aspects that promote the development of students' emotional intelligence. Students can learn to recognize emotions when they hear examples in the storytelling and determine how the characters demonstrate their emotional intelligence (Sulistianingsih et al. 2018). In turn, students learn to better care about their own needs, productively express and share their feelings, and empathize with others (Zarifsanaiey et al. 2022). The core of empathy is the art of listening, and being a good listener is essential for success in one's job (Goleman 1998).

Virtual Applications Promoting Engagement

In addition to personalized threaded discussion forums and digital storytelling, teachers can use other applications provided to them in their educational organization's LMS. Wikis or online databases, where students can collaboratively add to or edit the same document, can promote student participation. Similar engagement can be achieved outside of the LMS through the use of other online applications where students have access to the same web-based application or document. A wide variety of instructional tools and applications allow for real-time or asynchronous collaboration. Some may be available through the school or educational organization, while others may need to be purchased by the teacher.

No matter what activity or online application students engage in, teachers should involve students in a way that will promote conversation and interest. Teachers may find success in adapting the tools they use based on the strategies that each group responds to the best.

Questionnaires and Soliciting Feedback

As discussed, teachers need to involve parents and students in building the culture of the virtual classroom. One way to accomplish this is to ask parents and students to participate in a poll or survey to share their thoughts and provide constructive feedback. Through polls or questionnaires, teachers can connect with families, gain insights into what is happening in their virtual classrooms, support parents and students, and use what they discover to improve their teaching and lessons.

Poll or Questionnaire for the Course

STUDENT: [NAME]
1   What are you enjoying about our class? [student response]
2   What are you finding challenging about our class? [student response]

PARENT: [NAME]
1   What does your child need support in? [parent response]
2   What question(s) do you have for me? [parent response]

Ruedas-Gracia and coauthors (2022) discuss how leaders, like teachers, can be more effective when seeking feedback. They stress that people are poised to do their best work when they feel they belong to the group. Asking for feedback signals to students and their parents that the teacher is interested in them and their thoughts, giving families a sense of belonging.

In their study, Turner and Brannon (2022) discussed the feedback they received from their study participants:

> As she [the participant] said in one meeting, "I have never solicited so much feedback from students in my entire teaching career." Though she had always invited students to reflect on their skills and provide feedback on curriculum at the end of her units, as a result of her learning during this year, she began to ask them questions that were specific

to the pedagogical moves she made. As she grew to trust her students' feedback as a means to improve her practice during remote teaching, she saw the power it could have for her own learning and growth. (120)

According to Turner and Brannon (2022), it is not enough for teachers to reflect on their own teaching practices. They must reach out to their students and hear directly from them how they perceive their experience in the classroom. Teachers can then adjust their instruction as necessary to better fit their students and to grow as teachers. Instead of focusing on creating a virtual classroom *for* students, they should create the virtual classroom *with* students (Garcia et al. 2021). This approach reinforces a student-centered virtual classroom that elevates students and supports their emotional intelligence.

Another way for teachers to elicit timely feedback from students is to ask them to take the last five minutes of class to reflect on the lesson and complete an "exit card." The exit card information can be emailed to the teacher or simply submitted in the chat. Teachers can ask questions such as "Name three things you learned today in class" or "Tell me one word that describes how you are feeling right now." Teachers can also inquire what questions students still have or what more they would like to know about from the day's discussions.

Some teachers want greater feedback and may require their students to keep a journal that can be frequently shared with the teacher. Teachers should encourage students to express their thoughts in a way that engages them. Students who enjoy art can personalize their journals with sketches, and budding poets or musicians can add poems or music that demonstrate their learning.

Students also need objective, nonjudgmental feedback to improve, including when it comes to conflict or issues. When a problem arises, a teacher needs to calmly discuss what went wrong, why, and how to handle the situation if it arises again. By modeling and practicing appropriate behavior, teachers provide students with the vocabulary needed to regulate their emotions. Once students are able to process their emotions in this way, they can learn to manage those emotions by recognizing what they are feeling before they act upon it (Parrish 2018).

By receiving feedback and incorporating it into the virtual classroom, teachers are modeling how to integrate feedback into their lives (Garcia et al. 2021) and demonstrating that as teachers, they also participate in the learning process (Štibi et al. 2021). Students can see how teachers are learning and growing, even as adults. Furthermore, students continually receive feedback and are expected to adjust their way of doing things in response. What better way to promote their learning than by modeling that behavior?

Positive emotions modeled by teachers can promote the joy of learning within the classroom and have long-lasting effects on students (Pekrun 2014). Teachers can pass on their love of a particular subject, as well as their love of learning, through the enthusiasm and excitement they exude when teaching. That being said, teachers must be aware that, in addition to imparting knowledge to their students, they are also demonstrating leadership and serving as role models.

TEACHING TIPS

Question

When students are off topic in the webinar chat, what can I do while still supporting their emotional intelligence?

Answer

If students do not follow directions in the chat, teachers should respond in a way that supports their class culture. Teachers can begin by making blanket statements such as "Let's make sure we are following the directions in the chat." Making blanket statements gives students who are not following directions the opportunity to correct their behavior before being called out individually. Teachers can then provide students with guidance on what they can do to help, such as "Let's make sure everything we put in chat helps move our conversation forward."

Question

What can I do to help keep students on topic in the webinar chat while supporting their emotional intelligence?

Answer

To help students stay on topic in the webinar chat, teachers can verbally refer to what students are saying in chat. For example, if a student makes a comment that supports the lesson, the teacher would say the student's name out loud, repeat what the student said in the chat, and then comment on it. Teachers can also create an online game with the chat. For example, the teacher asks a question, the students write their response in the chat, the teacher counts down from three to one, and then as the teacher says, "Enter," the students all press "enter" at the same time. This allows everyone to think independently before sharing with the group.

CHAPTER 5

Assessing Academic and Emotional Progress in Online Learners

As a student, I always enjoy being able to pick the topics that I want to work on. One of the projects that I remember the most from high school was a chemistry research project where I got to choose the topic. It helped me learn more about that topic and more about what I wanted to do in my future career.

—PATRICK STEIN, online student

A Taxonomy of Student Skills

In 1956 the American educational psychologist Benjamin Bloom created a framework of six hierarchical cognitive skills focusing on student abilities: knowledge, comprehension, application, analysis, synthesis, and evaluation (Armstrong 2010). This framework provided teachers with a structure they could use to discuss learning outcomes and develop assessment methods. Many teachers have used Bloom's Taxonomy to offer students a variety of ways to demonstrate their knowledge of a subject through the creation of differentiated products.

A half-century later, Bloom's Taxonomy was revised to help teachers understand and implement standards-based curricula, in addition to helping them construct and analyze their own thinking. The revised skills are as follows: remembering, understanding, applying, analyzing, evaluating, and creating (Armstrong 2010). Although Bloom found different ways to measure *cognition*, he did not identify a way to measure *social ability* (Dweck 2006), so there remained a need for understanding how to assess relationship skills as part of emotional intelligence (Goleman 1995).

Checking for Understanding in the Webinar

Teachers can build relationships with their students by checking for understanding. At any point during the lesson, teachers can check in with students by stopping to ask them what questions they have. It is useful to give students enough time to formulate questions that they might not have asked otherwise and raise their hands. Giving students time to pause and reflect upon their learning can help lead to a deeper understanding of the material. By using the hierarchy of verbs in Bloom's Revised Taxonomy, teachers can encourage students to think deeper when responding—to go beyond just recalling information and instead to use information to analyze, evaluate, and create.

A teacher's emotional intelligence impacts their questioning technique. When asking questions, teachers need to cultivate self-awareness so they can in turn provide students with an opportunity for deeper self-reflection that can impact their thinking and new learning. Teachers should also keep their students' emotional intelligence in mind when posing questions. Some students may not feel comfortable asking for clarification or admitting when they do not understand something. They may need help learning how to ask questions, as well as help developing social awareness and moving from a reactive to a proactive mindset. To help students who are feeling self-conscious, the teacher can provide opportunities to ask questions outside the webinar room. For example, students could take part in online discussion boards and forums, where teachers can keep track of the students' input when assessing their participation in the course.

Checking for Understanding outside the Webinar

Outside of the webinar, the teacher can begin by establishing learning expectations through documents, such as the syllabus, and through assignment guidelines.

The idea is to provide clear, well-organized information that reflects the desired class culture. Step-by-step instructions with structured guidance, question-and-answer sessions, and regular check-ins will help keep students engaged and on track (Watson et al. 2017). This connectivity supports students in developing intrapersonal and interpersonal skills that will help them manage their emotions, thoughts, and behaviors as they strive to accomplish their goals.

Teachers can provide avenues of communication, such as through an email or a messaging system, to foster communication outside of the webinar room that will allow them to check students' understanding of class material. Martin and Bolliger (2018) found that study participants rated email reminders about assignments and other consistent notifications as the most important strategy to engage students with teachers. Some students feel anxious about sending a direct email to a teacher, especially if the student does not know the teacher well, is a younger student, or is not well versed in email communication. In such cases teachers can also suggest that parents send emails on their child's behalf.

Other methods of maintaining open communication with and between students might include message groups, chat features in the learning management system, and question-and-answer forums. Additionally, teachers can set up a questionnaire in the virtual classroom where students fill out the form to ask their questions. To respond, the teacher can send an email to the student, reply on a sheet that students can access, or post in the virtual classroom. No matter which communication methods are implemented, parents should have the ability to view the correspondence between their minor student and the teacher.

The Role of Assessments

Through assessments, teachers can gather information about what a student has learned and obtain daily data on students' readiness for particular ideas and skills, their interests, and their learning profiles (Tomlinson 1999). Assessments can be formative or summative. A formative assessment is diagnostic and can be based on discussions with the whole class, a small group, or an individual student. Summative assessment is evaluative and can be based on larger individual projects, such as student-created presentations, term papers, and videos. Because assessment informs instruction in a virtual classroom, it should be ongoing.

Teachers should give students opportunities for both formative and summative evaluation, in addition to asking them questions about the material they are studying. With good assessment in place, teachers can make informed decisions about how to address the needs of their students through supportive instruction, programs, and policies. Without good assessment, it is difficult for teachers to obtain a true reading on how well students are understanding the material and performing.

Formative Assessments

The type of formative assessment a teacher chooses to implement will depend on several factors, including the webinar room technology and the amount of time the teacher has with students. When an online class is synchronous, teachers can deliver direct instruction and check for understanding through formative assessments when meeting with students in the webinar room. Teachers who meet with their class synchronously multiple times a week for a longer period of time will have more opportunities to implement formative assessments, whereas teachers who meet with their students just once a week for a short period of time will need to tailor formative assessments to their situation.

The type of assessment will also depend on the ages and ability levels of students and on the relationships the students have with their teacher and with their classmates. Before having students work together in groups, teachers may choose to wait until rapport has been established between classmates.

Assessing students' comprehension and progress when teachers and students are not online simultaneously will work differently than in a live webinar. Working asynchronously provides students with time to dive into the material, re-engage with information that might be challenging, create projects, and answer questions. The extra time students have for asynchronous work gives teachers the ability to provide students with multiple ways to approach an assessment.

Teachers need to be mindful of the types of questions they ask during discussions and in asynchronous assessments. Instead of creating generic questions, teachers are encouraged to include realistic scenarios in their questions and prompts (Martin and Bolliger 2018). Including the students, and events important or relevant to them, can add to the realism and personalization of the situation.

In formative assessments, teachers should ask questions to check whether students understand the material and to identify what may need clarification. In both synchronous and asynchronous online discussions, teachers should use guiding prompts and questions (Martin and Bolliger 2018), which have been shown to be an important strategy for engaging students, cultivating their cognitive abilities, and deepening their comprehension (Gilbert and Dabbagh 2005). Whereas asking students closed-ended questions encourages students to respond in short, limited responses, asking higher-level, open-ended questions allows them to choose what they want to share and in how much detail, giving teachers an opportunity to better understand what their students comprehend.

Being familiar with different types of formative assessments will allow teachers to effectively choose or modify assessments before or during the webinar. If one type of formative assessment isn't working in a situation, the teacher can pivot to implementing another type, allowing them to use time in the webinar wisely.

When evaluating assessments, it may be beneficial for the teacher to keep track of student responses, how many times a specific student responds, or other criteria important to them. Recordkeeping can be done in a variety of ways, such as by using a spreadsheet, a physical notebook, an app from a third party, or the learning management system. Regardless of the technique implemented, the teacher should choose a method that works for them.

Using Polls and Games for Formative Assessment

Polls and games are other ways teachers can formatively assess and open the door for student discussion to measure growth.

Polling can be done by having students raise their hands or by using a webinar room's polling option, third-party app, or chat area. Sometimes, especially if a question is more personal, an anonymous poll is warranted and may produce more accurate results. Teachers can implement an anonymous poll via the webinar room's polling option or third-party app. Or, if an anonymous tool is not an option, students can prepare their responses in advance and share them directly with the teacher, who can use the results of the poll to launch a discussion.

Educational games in the webinar room can keep students interested, help students and teachers bond, and assist teachers in gauging students' level of understanding before, during, or after a session. Games might take the form of true-or-false questions, questions specific to the topic of the lesson, or something else the teacher creates. Teachers can prepare questions and answers ahead of time and then ask students to respond all at one time, to work in teams, or to share thoughts one at a time. After the students provide their responses, one or more class members or the teacher can elaborate and bring more clarity to the response. Formative assessment games played in the webinar room can be quick or can last the duration of the webinar time.

Although games can make learning fun, they can also lead to some strong emotions. It is useful for teachers to know whether their students are intrinsically or extrinsically motivated. Some students who are not externally motivated— that is, reward or goal oriented—may not enjoy participating in games or competitions and may not be motivated to win a trophy or prize. Additionally, some children may have to ease into playing a game, making this an opportune moment for teachers to ask for volunteers. Whatever formative assessment is chosen, teachers should keep in mind how the assessment will impact, and be impacted by, students' emotional intelligence.

Summative Assessments and Student Choice

Whereas formative assessments tend to be more closed-ended, with one main way to approach the topic, teachers can use summative assessments to give students choices about how to approach the assignment. Providing students with choices allows for more creativity and independence. The ability to choose can come in many forms. Choices can be simple, such what font color to use, or more complex, such as what project to create. Students who can make their own choices and address the topic in a way that works for them are building important emotional intelligence skills because they are emotionally connected to their learning (Dabrowski and Marshall 2018). Through this process, students become aware of their interests and strengths, which may not align with those of their classmates. They make their own decisions rather than doing what they are told to do and how they are to do it. Providing choice helps students gain self-confidence by giving them the freedom to approach complex thoughts and topics while minimizing their stress; it enables students to thrive and attain higher levels of success (Dabrowski and Marshall 2018; Dougherty et al. 2022).

Of course, summative assessments may include standardized tests and curriculum-based tests, which leave little room for modifications and personalizations. In a literature review of testing in the K–12 education system in the United States, Vinovskis (2019) stressed that standardized testing does not always lead to positive results because it can misrepresent student knowledge. Instead of relying on standardized testing alone, it is beneficial to give the students the ability to choose their focus or preferred method of assessment (Hawthorn-Embree et al. 2010; Milman 2020).

Assessment Formats in a Virtual Environment

Teachers should choose and develop course content and assessments that empower learners to discover and obtain proficiency in their learning (Stavredes and Herder 2014). Assessments and their variations will differ by level and subject matter. To ensure that the course proceeds smoothly, it is also important to be mindful of the limitations of the course design and course platform.

When building assessments for the virtual classroom, teachers may begin by understanding the rules and regulations of the overseeing school or educational organization. If teachers work independently, they need to be mindful of regional or national requirements or standards set by local, state, or country governments. For example, a science teacher should review a variety of standards, from national science standards to those set by independent scientific organizations. Awareness of and adherence to standards will support the quality of the online course and enable it to be used for academic credit in a number of contexts.

Teachers may create assessments in a threaded discussion in a learning management system. The teacher could post a central question, and the students' replies over time would create a thread. To give students the opportunity to personalize their experience, the teacher could pose multiple questions and offer students a choice, thereby creating a self-guided experience in a more engaging environment. Viewing others' work in a single-question forum can be boring for students because everyone may have a similar response. Reading others' thoughts in a multiple-question forum can be more exciting for students, who can think about perspectives on questions they hadn't considered previously. Adding flexibility and choices to the assignments in this way will help students adjust the assignments to fit their educational plan and help them take ownership of their learning (Dabrowski and Marshall 2018; Dougherty et al. 2022). Despite the benefits, asking more than one question in a forum involves additional work for the teacher when creating the lesson, and it is important that the assessments and choices provided to the student do not result in extra work for teachers in the long term.

In the short time, to provide students with choices, teachers can tap into their own creativity when constructing assessments for the virtual classroom. They can be creative with writing prompts—asking students to reply to a video, analyze a reading passage, or pretend to be a literary character or historical figure. They can also encourage students to create their own prompts, checking it with the teacher before devoting time and resources to exploring their idea.

If the teacher does not have access to a learning management system, an alternative is to give students the task of selecting a question to answer and using the webinar period to compose their answers. Then, students can either discuss each question as a class or participate in breakout groups to record their responses. If other platforms are not available, this assessment style could also be recreated in chat rooms via online documents and email.

Wikis, which commonly come standard with learning management systems, are applications that lend themselves to group projects, group discussions, or other collaborative endeavors. While some wikis allow teachers to see which students have contributed, many have greater restrictions and do not allow teachers to see who contributed. Other online projects, such as infographics, photo editing, and video production, allow students to tap into their creativity. Teachers may also choose to have shorter assignments due before the next webinar, or long-term assignments, such as research projects and in-depth video productions.

> Occasionally I do find that I need to rewrite assignments or include
> readings/videos at a lower level because I notice that I expected too high
> a level of understanding. The nice thing about the online environment is
> that it's easy to make adjustments like this, sometimes in real time.
> —SUKI WESSLING, online educator

Access to Resources

A school district or similar organization may provide students with technology, such as tablets or a computer, so everyone has access to the same resources. Schools and organizations might provide learning management systems, applications for word processing, or paid applications for students to create projects, such as virtual comic strip generators and presentation software.

Learning management systems usually come equipped with applications that can make it easy to create assessments like threaded discussions, quizzes, and assignments where students cannot see others' responses. However, some systems can be challenging and time consuming to use. For example, a system may have a quiz-making module that presents students with a set of questions and then automatically grades their responses. This type of assessment requires the teacher to create the quiz ahead of time and input all the possible answers to each question. When creating a quiz like this, teachers should include a copy of the questions and answers in a document on their computer for easy reference and to guard against future file corruption. Opportunities for alternative questions and responses can be beneficial, but quizzes should not be used as the main assessment tool, as they do not promote student creativity and exploration.

When working independently from a school or organization in an online environment, teachers need to be mindful that some students will not have the same access to technology as their classmates. As a result, educators who lack access to that technical infrastructure may need to design assessments in more creative ways, choosing assignments that students can easily complete using whatever technology or resources they have available.

One alternative to paid services consists of free online resources. These free resources can be beneficial in the short term, but sometimes computer applications that start out as free services later change to paid services. Free online resources may also go out of business or have inadequate support systems. It is a good idea for teachers to keep copies of their assignments in a readable format on their computers to avoid losing their information later. When using an online resource, teachers should look into the company's business practices and potential for longevity. Building assessments around established applications can minimize the potential need to recreate assignments later.

Hands-On Activities

Oftentimes, families think that students will miss out on hands-on activities if they are learning online. This is not always the case. It is true that engaging in hands-on activities at home can be challenging, especially if families do not have the means to get the necessary resources, such as laboratory equipment for a college-level chemistry class. In many situations, however, hands-on activities can be incorporated into online learning.

If families from the general public are enrolling in classes, the teacher should let them know ahead of time about extra expenses that may be incurred. Up-front communication allows families to budget funds to cover extra expenses and helps ensure that students do not feel excluded as a result of their socioeconomic status.

Sometimes teachers request an extra fee to cover required items that they purchase and send to students. Teachers should allow sufficient time for these items to arrive before any assignments require these materials. Being proactive about expenses and helping families procure hands-on resources supports both the student and their family.

Creating hands-on activities at home can also be a challenge for families whose children need extra support. Therefore, it is important to be flexible with assessment expectations (Ruecker 2021). Providing students with assignment alternatives, allowing for individual modifications, and offering support where needed can positively impact students' emotional intelligence.

Students Sharing Their Work

Students can share their completed larger projects in a variety of ways—by, for instance, presenting their project during the webinar, posting a picture, or creating a video presentation. No matter what mode the student chooses, their choice should reflect their ability and their situation, and teachers should be mindful of students' feelings about sharing work with the class. Forcing students to share their projects or share any information publicly should be avoided (Beeman 2022).

Not all students feel comfortable sharing their projects or other work with the group for a variety of reasons, including difficulty speaking publicly, fear of how they will be perceived, and feelings of inadequacy (Beeman 2022). Teachers can help their students feel more comfortable by easing them into the sharing process over time. The rapport teachers create with their students, the relationships students build with each other, and the promotion of the classroom culture are all components that help quieter students gain self-confidence to share in class (Beeman 2022; Frisby and Martin 2010).

It can be difficult to assess a fearful student's knowledge if the assessment is based on speaking in class. Teachers might start the year by asking students individually about their comfort level when it comes to public speaking or group work. By determining and working to understand their students' level of comfort, teachers can work to alleviate their fears (Frisby and Martin 2010).

Discussions with parents may reveal a desire for their child to work on certain skills, such as public speaking or ability to work in groups. Teachers may want to start a conversation with parents about the child's educational goals or aspirations at home before involving the child in the conversation. Parents, teachers, and children are all important elements of a child's education. Although the parent and teacher may agree, it is important for the student's voice to be heard and for parents, teachers, and students all to work together (Westerberg et al. 2020). A teacher might find it challenging to focus on a student's individual needs when the learning environment includes specific rules and regulations, but being mindful of the student's emotional intelligence will benefit that student in the long run.

Making Accommodations

If a student is reluctant to complete a certain task, determining the root cause of the feeling can help students better understand themselves and identify a path forward. Although teachers can find it difficult to work with students who lack motivation or are fearful about moving beyond their comfort zone, teachers can nurture emotional intelligence in these students by helping them become aware of and understand their way of managing emotions and how it affects others. Working with the student in this way can give them the skills needed not only to address the current situation but also to build social and emotional skills to tackle future challenges.

Assignments that are out of a student's comfort zone, like public speaking or working with a group, can be stressful. Of course, stressful assignments are not confined to activities traditionally perceived as stressful—students can perceive anything as stressful, such as being required to respond to a classmate's post. Every student is different and has different concerns. Mindfully assisting students in approaching assignments that cause them stress can benefit the students and allow them to grow past this worry (Frisby and Martin 2010).

Sometimes, teachers can alter the assignment to accommodate a student or situation. If a student is reluctant to present in front of the class, they might choose to record their presentation and play back the recording to the class. This modification enables the student to complete the assignment without the stress of public speaking. Other modifications would need to be made if the course is on public speaking, but recording the presentation might be a first step in helping the student feel more comfortable in such a setting.

Events and situations outside of the classroom may also impact students and require classroom plans and assignments to be altered. Concessions can be made on an individual basis or for the group as a whole. If a student experiences the death of someone important to them, the teacher may elect to cover an event like 9/11 at a later time. It is important for students to feel comfortable sharing information that may impact their learning with the teacher so the teacher has the opportunity to act or react accordingly. Ensuring that students feel comfortable enough to communicate this way with the teacher underlines the need for a supportive class culture (Beeman 2022).

Rubrics as Assignment Feedback

Some schools and educational organizations have a grading system or scale that teachers must use for assessment. Other organizations and instructors rely solely on written feedback rather than traditional grades. In the latter situation, teachers may want to assess student work using a system that can translate to a percentage grade on a set grading scale for families accustomed to a regular grading system, who may find it challenging to switch to a class where student performance isn't graded.

A more flexible assessment tool is a rubric, which can help teachers grade open-ended assessments that require students to integrate their interests and abilities in their projects. Martin and Bolliger (2018) reported that, after email reminders, providing students with grading rubrics for course assignments was the second most important strategy in engaging students with teachers, according to students. Rubrics have been shown to be effective when assessing online assignments (Gayton and McEwen 2007). Over time, teachers have also become increasingly interested in creating and using formative assessments and rubrics to develop and nurture their students' social-emotional skills.

Rubrics have been found to allow for more accurate evaluation of student ability than other methods (Bali and Ramadan 2007). Efffective rubrics include "clear performance criteria, structured writing, a deep approach to learning, and a better analysis and application of subject content knowledge" (Mphahlele 2022, 12). When used appropriately, rubrics can be differentiated to address various ability groups within a class. For example, a rubric might offer an exemplary learning level for grading gifted children to address their unique learning needs. It might also provide evidence-based guidelines for assessing social-emotional dimensions, such as creativity and critical thinking.

Although rubrics have been an established practice for years, they are not always used effectively (Mphahlele 2022; Panadero and Jönsson 2020). Rubrics need to be clear and easy to understand so that students—and instructional staff—can easily interpret them (Gayton and McEwen 2007). Providing students with too much information on a rubric can cause the rubric to become closed and stifling, leading students to focus on the rubric instead of on the task. Rather than allowing creativity to flow and feeling excitement about the learning process, the student may pay attention to how many sentences they have written or how many adjectives they have used. Leaving the rubric as open as possible may help the student focus on the task at hand.

The table shows an example of an open rubric that places the focus on the assignment and is used by many teachers at Athena's Advanced Academy, Inc. The qualitative descriptions in this scale can be translated to quantitative letter grades, with an A being "Complete!" and an F being "Incomplete."

By using a broad rubric like this, teachers can focus on being creative with assignments rather than ensuring the assignment fits the rubric or modifying the rubric to fit the assignment. Once students are aware of a generalized rubric with broad criteria, they know what to expect and can focus on the assignment, giving them the freedom to tap into their creativity.

Because this rubric is subjective, it cannot be used in all situations. It can, however, serve as a measure that focuses on the learning process while providing students with a grade. Similar rubrics can be used with a variety of activities, including peer assessment exercises (Mphahlele 2022). Rubrics are also a useful way to assess social-emotional learning because they offer concrete and behaviorally oriented criteria that facilitate students' self-reflection about where they are and where they want to be (Panadero and Jönsson 2020).

The beauty of using a rubric loosely based on grades is that it can easily shift students' and parents' focus from the achievement of a grade to the learning taking place. Students frequently fixate on a grade instead of on learning, and society often focuses on obtaining a grade to demonstrate mastery. Grades have a place in helping teachers and parents understand what the student has learned, but it is important to balance the use of grades with the love of learning.

Open Rubric Example

GRADE	EXPLANATION
Complete!	All basic instructions were followed, and the student's work showed evidence of effort and understanding.
Satisfactory	Nearly all instructions were followed, but something was missing. The student's work shows satisfactory effort and understanding.
Partially Complete	Most instructions were followed, but there were multiple omissions. The student's work shows some effort and understanding.
Attempted	Some instructions were followed. The student's work shows minimal effort and understanding.
Incomplete	Instructions were not followed. The student's work does not show effort or understanding.

Source: Athena's Advanced Academy, Inc.

Feedback and Emotional Intelligence

Feedback from teachers to students falls into two categories: feedback on the gap in performance—the negative aspects of their work—and feedback on the positive outcomes and effort (Faulconer et al. 2022). Because feedback can evoke negative emotions and put an individual on the defensive, it needs to be presented in a positive, empathetic, and constructive way to enhance communication and encourage personal growth. For teachers, providing feedback with emotional intelligence is an important tool they can use to help students learn and improve.

Students receiving feedback based only on their gap in performance experience lower confidence and self-esteem when it came to their academic performance. In addition, feedback that is focused on the gap in performance, vague, unrelated to the assessment, or lacking in guidance fails to improve student learning (Weaver 2006).

Daniel Goleman cautions that it is best to keep one's emotions in balance and have empathy when delivering tough feedback. Great leaders have strengths in emotional intelligence as well as in their abilities and skills in areas such as integrity and strategic thinking (Goleman 2023). As leaders in the classroom, it is critical that teachers lead with consideration and empathy. They must think about any relevant aspects of a student's personal life that could influence how the feedback being provided could be interpreted.

One study discovered that student perceptions of an online course did not change when feedback was based on their gap in performance. In contrast, when students were provided with both gap-in-performance feedback and positive reinforcement, their grades rose an entire letter grade on average, suggesting that including both kinds of feedback boosted students' learning in an online setting. Teachers' feedback should thus include both areas for improvement and positive feedback about students' work (Faulconer et al. 2022).

Other research shows that providing feedback on student work can shift students either toward or away from a growth mindset and self-confidence. Focusing on strengths and areas for improvement—in a positive light—can go a long way toward stimulating a positive sense of self-worth and keeping students engaged with the course (Alharbi and Alqefari 2022).

Mastering the strategy of giving feedback in an online course makes a considerable difference in student satisfaction and retention (Kim and Moore 2005). Feedback should be provided early and often. Feedback on particular assignments is often more private, and because it is customized, it can shape a student's growth (Boettcher and Conrad 2010). Feedback from their classmates can also help to foster engagement. According to Kim and Moore (2005), opportunities for student feedback result in satisfaction and good feelings about the course.

Feedback for Teachers

One of a teacher's responsibilities is helping students take charge of their education and develop autonomy. For students to maintain and improve their emotional intelligence, they need to be aware of their learning and comfort level in the class, and they may have feedback for teachers in this regard. By checking in with students and parents, teachers can gain an understanding of their perspectives, experiences, and expectations; this can be accomplished in a variety of ways.

Providing students with self-reflective survey questions to answer outside of the webinar will give them time to reflect on their experience in class and give the teacher student-specific feedback (Suyatno et al. 2021). Teachers could choose to give students a check-in form early in the course so that changes and adjustments can be made. Students are often given teacher evaluation forms at the end of a course, when it is too late for the teacher to rectify any problems.

Some school systems may require parent-teacher meetings in a webinar room or threaded discussion. Regardless of the mode of communication, the student should be included in the conversation so they have the opportunity to take ownership of their learning (Dabrowski and Marshall 2018; Dougherty et al. 2022).

Although it is not always easy to do, teachers should follow up with students who provide feedback to help keep those students engaged (Sutherland et al. 2019). Teachers should use the information they gather to fine-tune the class experience for their students. They can either make adjustments for the whole group or work with individual students to modify the curriculum.

To support struggling students, the teacher can email them directly while copying their parents. The email should reflect the established tone of the virtual classroom—focusing on the positive and then addressing the issue. After the root issue has been addressed, the teacher can give ideas on how to move forward. Sending an email to parents and students who are not struggling will let them know that their response was received. Letting parents know the student is happy and well adjusted can help solidify the teacher-parent relationship (Ruedas-Gracia et al. 2022).

For teachers who are required to conduct parent-teacher conferences, information gathered through student surveys can be invaluable. Showing a correlation between a student's responses on the survey and their assessment grades can assist teachers and parents when they are creating a plan to address any goals or concerns.

Social-Emotional Assessments

To better understand their students' social and emotional intelligence, teachers often turn to social and emotional assessments. Teachers and schools increasingly recognize the need for reliable and valid assessment tools for social-emotional learning. Without assessment tools, schools cannot gather the data they need to make informed decisions about the development of a child's emotional intelligence.

Although some social-emotional learning assessments exist, few serve the full range of purposes, from formative assessment to accountability, and of levels, from prekindergarten through high school. Teachers should familiarize themselves with what is available so they can learn appropriate uses and limits. McKown (2017) states that we need to invest significant resources if we want to get serious about assessing social-emotional learning.

Many empirically sound scales exist to provide tools that measure emotional intelligence. O'Connor and coauthors (2019) provide an overview of scales for researchers and practitioners that range from self-reported emotional intelligence tests to inventory and situational tests of management and understanding. Teachers will find it worthwhile to search online for companies that offer resource books and social-emotional learning kits for their classrooms.

Product Assessments

Assessments can include a variety of teacher-initiated or student-designed products that show the student's development and mastery of a subject. The selected product assessments can range from simple to complicated, but they should be appropriate for the student's age, grade, and experience: say, a diorama for a primary school student or a sophisticated research project for a high school student.

Renzulli and Callahan (2008) argue that product assessment is an authentic way to assess real learning. Teachers should decide whether they want to use their own assessments or those that already meet technical adequacy. In making this choice, teachers need to ensure that these tools promote student individuality and personal growth. No matter which assessments or evaluation tools are used, they should reflect the class culture and support students' emotional intelligence.

TEACHING TIP

Question

How can I provide my reluctant students with more choices when they are required to create presentations?

Answer

It can be challenging for some students to reach the point where they feel comfortable giving a presentation. To help them get there, teachers can provide students with the option of creating a silent presentation. The reluctant learner would create a presentation consisting of words on slides. In class, the student's classmates could read the presentation to themselves. If students are required to present orally, students could prerecord themselves giving the presentation and present the recording to the class.

CHAPTER 6

Involving Parents in the Virtual Learning Experience

> My goal is to empower the parent. Parents know their child, their educational goals for the child, and their child's unique needs best.
> —VALERIE NANDOR, PhD, online educator

Child Safety Concerns

When a child is born, parents feel an overwhelming urge to protect them—a quick scroll through online catalogs of baby supplies shows manufacturers, in response to this urge, trumpeting the safety features of their products. Of course, parents aren't concerned just about their child's physical well-being—they are also focused on protecting their child's mental health and educational growth. But, even with all of the protective measures in place, parents aren't always able to keep their child safe.

Besides wanting to protect their child from circumstances beyond their control, parents frequently worry about the things they can control. They often question their own decisions and focus on how those decisions—from seemingly simple choices about what clothes to purchase to more complex decisions like choosing the best educational environment—impact their child's life. Making these decisions can be overwhelming and can affect parenting styles.

Parenting Styles

Parents differ in how they relate to and treat their children. Whether they are laissez-faire or strict, parents should be available to their children and use opportunities to coach them. Children benefit from chances to develop their abilities to identify, manage, and harness their emotions and increase their capacity for empathy in various situations (Goleman 1995).

When parents feel emotionally out of control, their difficulty can manifest itself in one or more of the following ways:

- They feel the emotion (anger, sadness, or fear).
- They believe they feel it too intensely.
- They have trouble calming down after experiencing intense feelings.
- They become disorganized and have trouble functioning when they feel the emotion.
- They hate the way they behave when they are feeling the emotion.
- They are always on guard against the feeling.
- They find themselves acting neutral (calm, understanding, sympathetic), but it's only an act.
- They believe the feeling is destructive and even immoral.
- They feel they need help with the emotion. (Gottman 1997, 78–79)

Often, parents who experience feeling out of control compensate by hiding their emotions from their child (Gottman 1997). Unfortunately, a lack of authentic communication can be detrimental to the child, who misses an opportunity to learn how to deal with real emotions when solving problems. By labeling and validating all types of emotions, parents can help their child understand the child's own feelings, normalize these feelings, and develop empathy.

Parental Concerns about Online Learning

Parents often have fears when it comes to their child learning virtually (Zhao et al. 2020). One of the biggest is online safety. Parents need to be assured that the teacher they are sending their child to is someone they can trust, someone who will not harm the child. Trust does not come easily, so it is important for teachers to be patient and consistent while working on building trusting relationships with parents so they can work together to support the student (Asih et al. 2022).

Parents also have concerns about their child's privacy online (Davis et al. 2021). To address this fear, teachers and virtual schools can provide information to parents on how their child will be kept safe while participating in virtual classes. This information can be shared at the beginning of each course and reinforced over time.

There is a perception that teachers need to focus only on their students, but that is not the case. Teachers also have to work with their students' parents, especially when children are young. To guide their communications with families concerning a child's emotional intelligence, teachers need to ask themselves questions, such as the following (Tantillo Philibert and Slade 2022, 80):

- How often do I ask families what is going on at home that could impact (positively or negatively) student interaction in class?
- What feedback do I provide to families on student dispositions in the areas of self-awareness, self-regulation, social awareness, and responsible decision-making?
- How do families know my classroom expectations for student engagement, academic, and social-emotional learning (SEL)? How do I help families set goals for their child in SEL, alongside the goals they have for academic growth and achievement?
- Do families communicate their needs with me? Why or why not? How could we facilitate additional two-way communication that benefits all?

Emotional Intelligence of Parents

The emotional intelligence of parents, like that of students, varies and manifests itself in different ways. Some parents want to be involved in every aspect of their child's learning while others have a more hands-off approach. No matter what parenting style is present, the child is impacted by their parent's level of involvement.

Parents bring years of their own educational experiences to the table when they first meet teachers, and this history affects both their own and their child's emotional intelligence. A teacher's first contact with a family is often through the student's parents (Asih et al. 2022; Muirhead 2000). Given their desire to keep their child safe and to protect their well-being, parents may approach the relationship with the teacher cautiously.

Parents may have only minimal information about the teacher before their child enters the virtual classroom. The initial information will depend on the situation. Independent teachers may have their own websites and social media platforms and be associated with larger online organizations. Before classes begin, parents can research the teacher through an internet search and obtain information to help them decide whether the teacher is a good fit for their child. In contrast, a teacher working with an established virtual school may not have the same individual online presence as a teacher working independently. Established online schools may only have the teachers' names posted on the school's website. Teachers in this situation can rely on the school's reputation as well as their own. In both situations, teachers are required to build relationships with the parents of the students in their classes.

Although the student is the focus in the virtual classroom, teachers should keep in mind that a student's emotional intelligence is impacted by what occurs at home. Children, particularly those learning online, often spend a lot of time at home with their parents, so they are typically heavily influenced by their parents and others in their household and community. Thus, the emotional intelligence of the parents can impact the child and can become a factor when it comes to supporting the child's educational growth (Simorangkir et al. 2022). Even if parents are confident that their child's teacher is a competent instructor who is there to help them, they may still feel anxious, and those anxious feelings may carry over to their child. Conversely, a child's anxious feelings may impact the way the parent relates to the teacher.

It is not the teacher's responsibility to provide support for family and home life. Recognizing, however, that their students are greatly impacted by what goes on at home can assist teachers when corresponding and working with students and their parents. As the teacher, it is important to lead by example and maintain a calm and steady presence. By communicating that they want the very best for the student, teachers can work together with parents as partners in a child's education. Creating a supportive educational environment that involves parents can bring everyone together to support the child's learning while alleviating anxious feelings (Asih et al. 2022).

Ideally, parents should support and promote their child's emotional intelligence to give them the tools they need to grow up and mature into adults with highly developed emotional intelligence skills (Ounprasertsuk and Suksatan 2021). It is important, therefore, for parents to have information on, and an understanding of, the developmental learning and growth expectations for their child, including social-emotional, to ensure that the home and school environments work as one during virtual learning (Tantillo Philibert and Slade 2022).

Communicating with Parents

Including parents in the correspondence with and about their child can help improve the student-parent-teacher relationship (Ruedas-Gracia et al. 2022). Teachers can approach parents by viewing them as an extension of their child, while keeping in mind that the family as a whole can support the student's emotional intelligence (Simorangkir et al. 2022). By intentionally keeping parents well informed, teachers are working with the emotional intelligence abilities not only of their students, but also of their students' parents.

Early in the introduction phase, the teacher should establish learning goals and objectives for a set of clearly articulated high expectations for the class. Knowing the expectations before the class begins helps put students' and parents' minds at ease.

Regular and ongoing communication—through the LMS, email, video conferencing, text, or phone—is highly encouraged. Once communication has been established, the mode of communication should be maintained. It can be difficult for parents to know where to look for correspondence if the teacher is communicating through the learning management system one week and through email the next.

Teachers should also establish a schedule of communication with parents. Depending on the length and format of a class, the teacher may decide to email a newsletter to parents about what students are learning once a week or every three weeks. No matter the frequency of communication, conveying a communication plan will create a positive connection upon which parents can rely (Westerberg et al. 2020).

A newsletter may not only contain general information but also explain nuances of the course or coursework. When sending out class information, the teacher may include learning resources for parents to peruse with students that will support what is being taught in class. If a parent has a question about the class, the teacher may share the answer with all the parents so everyone has the same information, but the teacher should not identify the original parent by name unless given express permission. Teachers might suggest activities parents could do with their children, such as field trips, to dive deeper into the subject matter. They can also offer parents strategies to support their child's success in the classroom.

In addition to communicating with parents about the course as a whole, teachers will find it beneficial to communicate with specific parents about their child. Individualized communication can help parents better understand where their child is in their learning and what is needed as they progress through the course. Teachers should share regular feedback on how the child is progressing in class or what can be done to help them improve. Sometimes an LMS can provide information parents need with a click of a button. Other times, specific emails are warranted. No matter which modes of communication are used, there should be a way for parents to learn about their child's academic as well as social-emotional development.

To further build relationships with parents, teachers might set up parent-teacher conferences, even if they are not a requirement of the school or organization where the class is being taught. These online conferences may be as simple or complex as desired. Teachers may email uploaded files to parents beforehand or provide links to full reports at the conference. They may want to involve the student in the conference by asking them to share and explain a project or piece of work. Participation by students can instill confidence and empower them to take responsibility for their learning.

In lieu of a parent-teacher conference, teachers might email a questionnaire to parents (and students) to gauge how they perceive the class and the child's progress. These questionnaires may be elaborate, asking several questions about the class, or simple, one-question questionnaires to provide parents and students with another avenue to ask questions. For example, the questionnaire could consist of just the question "Is there anything you want to ask me about the class?" Sometimes everyone needs encouragement to ask questions.

Student-Parent-Teacher Relationship

Working with parents and families can be stressful for teachers. Since teachers have the added responsibility of engaging with different levels of parental emotional intelligence, there is potential for animosity toward parents to fester. Although the focus in the virtual classroom isn't on the emotional intelligence levels of parents, the teacher-parent relationship can impact the effectiveness, as well as the mental well-being, of the teacher (Farmer 2020). Ideally, therefore, teachers should seek to develop a strong working relationship with parents early on to foster a positive, healthy, working partnership.

Teachers can nurture the student-parent-teacher relationship by asking parents to share their hopes and expectations for their child and involving them in the child's education. Some parents may want their child to simply learn more than what they knew before the class began. Others may want to focus on certain skills, such as public speaking.

Knowing the parents' expectations up front can assist teachers in making sure the expectations are addressed. This information can be helpful, especially if the class does not include their particular goal. Once teachers learn about this expectation, they can address it and discuss other ways to support the parent's expectation for their child. It is important for parents to realize that although a teacher may encourage their student to participate, it is ultimately up to the student to take part. Setting realistic goals with parents can help align everyone's expectations to provide the child with the best chance of success in the classroom.

Teachers need to take time to celebrate positive classroom moments and achievements. Focusing on the positive rather than the negative can foster the relationship between the student and teacher as well as between the parent and teacher. Teachers must be mindful of informing parents of their child's social-emotional effort and growth in celebration of the whole child.

Parents need to understand their child's developmental growth expectations in all subject areas, including social-emotional, and this information can be conveyed in the form of a whole-child report card. By respecting and sharing a student's self-awareness, self-management, and social awareness skills in addition to their self-efficacy abilities, teachers will encourage parents to support the emotional intelligence of their child at home. They can remind parents that all parenting battles aren't won with reason and logic alone; they also require awareness and empathy. Giving parents the chance to engage in an open dialogue with teachers can improve their empathy for their child (Tantillo Philibert and Slade 2022). To be emotionally intelligent, parents must manage their own emotions and foster healthy emotional development in their children (Singhal 2021).

Both parents and teachers know different things about a child (Tomlinson 1999). Therefore, it is important to the education of the whole child that both parents and teachers collaborate and learn from one another. By providing opportunities for parents to become involved with their child's online learning, teachers can develop a partnership with parents in which both gain a deeper insight into the educational development of the child.

Parents as Emotional Coaches

A person's own experiences and upbringing influence how they raise their children and in turn affects the emotional intelligence of those children. By being cognizant of and receptive to their children's feelings, parents can assume the role of an emotional coach. Many parents, however, may have to overcome their own emotional barriers that result from the way emotions were managed when they were growing up. Nonetheless, people from all cultural backgrounds can demonstrate sensitivity to the feelings of their children (Gottman 1997).

Research reveals that children who feel loved and respected in their families tend to show respect for others and perform better in school (Lickona 2021). Thus, it is important for parents to develop their ability to consciously foster, convey, and exemplify an environment of compassion and understanding at home by staying tuned in to their child's everyday needs as they grow (Gottman 1997). By recognizing the importance of relating to their child through emotions, parents also build common ground for solving problems together. Gottman (1997, 75) identifies five steps, presented below, through which parents can build empathy into relationships with their children to enhance their emotional intelligence, and teachers may wish to communicate this information to parents.

Parents as Emotional Coaches

1   Be aware of the child's emotions.

2   Recognize emotion as an opportunity for intimacy and teaching.

3   Listen empathically and validate the child's feelings.

4   Help the child verbally label emotions.

5   Set limits while helping the child problem-solve.

Engaging Parents as Partners

Engaging parents as partners in their child's education will depend on such factors as the child's needs, age, and ability level. The amount of interest parents take in their child's work may vary widely, from being uninterested and disengaged to being overbearing and overinvolved. The goal is to find the perfect level of interest and involvement for the child so parents are working with the teacher while giving the teacher the space they need to do their job.

Instead of viewing the student as the only stakeholder in the situation, teachers should view the parents as an extension of the child who should be involved in the educational process (Asih et al. 2022). To do this, teachers can modify many of the strategies and techniques for engaging students to also include parents. For example, teachers can invite parents to take an active role in their classroom by working with students in chat rooms—mentoring students who are working on independent study projects, expanding discussions with advanced readers, or reviewing concepts with struggling or reluctant learners. If teachers hold office hours, they can encourage parents to attend and ask questions.

Teachers can include parents in their emails or correspondence with students. This is especially recommended when children are younger and need assistance with responding to the teacher. For older children who need practice with autonomy (the motivating power of being able to do things on one's own), including parents on emails may be warranted only when issues arise. The level of communication may depend on the functionality of the LMS platform. Some LMS platforms include a way for the system to automatically send out progress reports or information about upcoming due dates to parents, whereas other systems do not.

Working with parents to help their children gain autonomy may prove to be challenging for teachers. At some point, a developmental transition needs to occur so that the child can become an independent learner. Teachers can support parents by offering their children choice and independence in finding meaningful solutions. Supporting children to find meaningful solutions on their own will help them navigate their world and develop responsibility (David 2016).

If the parent is particularly protective of their child, online education can be helpful. In a virtual class, a parent can be in the background or next to the student (preferably out of camera range if the camera is on), supporting their student.

Of course, if a parent is present in the background of a webinar, that parent will be monitoring the teacher as well as the class. If the parent expresses criticism of the teacher, curriculum, or teaching style, the teacher should employ the same tools they use when working with students: attempt to understand their perspective and provide recommendations and support. By viewing this as a teachable moment, teachers can remain calm and receptive to trying to understand how the parent feels. Being skillful in managing their own emotions, and remaining empathetic, helps teachers to help parents manage theirs. Empathy is at the foundation of a relationship (Goleman 1995).

Helping Parents Feel Connected

Helping parents feel connected to their child's learning process can contribute to a positive mental state for the student. Parents can extend their child's learning by reading with them, playing educational games, and taking them on trips to expose them to art, music, and nature. Teachers can encourage parents to volunteer to help out with virtual activities or invite them to be guest speakers in a course webinar. As previously discussed, teachers can also provide parents with information on emotional coaching as a supportive way to help students find meaningful solutions and develop the autonomy to navigate their world (David 2016).

Assisting the parent in helping their child at home is a way to support the student's emotional intelligence. Oftentimes, parents are unsure about how to achieve a healthy parenting relationship that helps their child get the most out of the online experience. To alleviate that uncertainty, teachers can share ideas and helpful hints on ways to set up an effective learning environment at home. Specifically, they can offer

- tips for positive communication,
- techniques for active listening,
- tools for building self-esteem and self-confidence,
- strategies for healthy eating and sleeping habits, and
- practices for mindfulness and stress reduction.

Teachers may add information that addresses fears parents may have about learning online. These fears may include

- concern about whether their child will receive a quality and academically appropriate education online,
- concern about their child's relationship with the online teacher,
- concern about the level of communication between parents and teachers,
- concern that the way the class is structured won't work for their child,
- concern regarding the online educational environment and the connection between students,
- concern about the social interaction between students, and
- concern about the technology used in the virtual class (Stein 2013).

Some of these concerns can be addressed before the class begins. For example, a parent may worry that their child will not know how to use the virtual classroom technology or will not be able to find the webinar room. Providing parents with information on how to navigate the technology may reduce their anxiety and ensure that they can help their child if needed (Rathaliya et al. 2022). Other concerns, such as worry over the social interaction between students, will require more time to address. However, communicating the parameters of the class and fostering a culture based on emotional intelligence will help ease fears over time (Westerberg et al. 2020).

Any opportunities to involve parents in the virtual learning experience will depend on the type of school and class. For all-encompassing, yearlong online schools, teachers can facilitate groups that support parents and, in turn, students. Teachers at smaller organizations can also set up groups, but parents may not become as actively involved, especially if the student is attending only one or two classes.

Parent Involvement in the Online Classroom

Teachers can offer parents a wide range of ways to become involved in their child's online classroom:

- *Parent mentoring.* Parents of former students can be available to answer questions and give support to parents new to the school or organization. A mentoring program may give new parents another place to turn with questions, especially if they do not feel comfortable asking the teacher. A parent mentor can be trained to let the teacher know if their attention is warranted.

- *Parent discussion groups and parent-teacher discussion groups.* A discussion group gives parents the opportunity to meet with others who are going through the same virtual classroom experience. For example, parents of students in a physics class can meet to discuss how to help their child through the course. If the discussion group does not include the teacher, the parent leader should be instructed to let the teacher know if their attention to a topic or problem is warranted. If the discussion group includes the teacher, parents can ask the teacher broad questions about the course. The information provided in the session can additionally be emailed or sent out in a newsletter. These groups can be formal or informal (e.g., a virtual chat over coffee) and held in a variety of ways, including via webinars or chat groups on a virtual platform or app.

- *Social media parent groups.* Like mentoring and discussion groups, social media groups can allow parents to connect with parents of students who have already taken part in the virtual class, thereby creating a larger community and long-term connections.

- *Parent-student-teacher clubs.* Sometimes the key to unlocking involvement, communication, and positive interactions is to meet in a less formal setting involving parents and students. The parties may enjoy bonding in an online book club that includes a lively discussion based on a connection to what their child is learning in class. A club could also be formalized and opened up to families of individuals in other classes. Teachers could work together to combine the clubs and unite the groups if they have a relationship with other online teachers who teach in different classes, schools, or organizations.

- *Parent workshops or resource center.* Besides emailing tips and tricks to help parents support their child, teachers can hold workshops that offer guidance and solutions for parents. Topics may include virtual learning, how to navigate the LMS, how to help their child with homework, and how to support their child's academic and social-emotional growth.

- *Communication log.* When appropriate or applicable, teachers can keep a record of the regular communication between parents and teachers in an accessible communication log. There, parents can access all the notes and messages from the teacher to ensure that they haven't missed any important information. Teachers could include this log in the LMS or another virtual application or place it on a class website or blog dedicated to the class.

- *Video tutorials.* Video tutorials for parents may foster a greater connection between parents and teachers, especially if parents are given the opportunity to see the teacher face to face or hear their voice. Topics might include classroom procedures and tips on helping your child stay focused, building your child's self-confidence, and helping your child manage their emotions.

In addition to helping teachers connect with parents, these ideas can be modified to engage students. For example, as mentioned earlier, teachers who teach in webinars with no video component can connect with students visually by recording and sharing a video of themselves providing feedback, instructions, or other messages. Students might be given the opportunity to respond in a video of themselves. Please note that permission to have a recorded likeness of a student posted anywhere online should be approved by their parents.

Displaying Student Work

Displaying student work online is one way teachers can highlight the positive accomplishments of student learning. Student work can be shared internally in the LMS or externally through mailing lists and social media. It might also be integrated in online lessons to instill pride, motivate learning, and share achievements.

Caution should be used when handling a student's personal information, including the student's name and physical description, especially when the content is available to the public online. Teachers should obtain student and parental permission before sharing any information about the student. When reaching out to parents and students to obtain permission to post student work, teachers might suggest alternatives to the student's photo, such as a photo of something they enjoy, a place they've been, or a pet. Instead of posting their full name, students might choose to use their first name and last initial, first name only, or initials only or could remain anonymous when sharing their work. Teachers must ensure that when publicly posted, the work itself does not contain any identifying information, such as the student's name or likeness.

Word of Caution

In some situations, the information, tips, and support teachers can provide are not enough to help families meet the educational needs of their students. It is then important that the teacher is proactive in recommending further intervention (e.g., a reading specialist or pediatric therapist). When this happens, having a preestablished supportive relationship with the student's parents may make the difficult situation easier and lead to a positive change in the student's life.

TEACHING TIPS

Question

What can I do to support parents when their child has a meltdown over schoolwork?

Answer

A child's meltdown is an opportune time to develop the parent's understanding of emotional intelligence. Encourage the parent to take a deep breath, regain emotional control, and refrain from reacting angrily to their child's misbehavior. Remind them of the airline instruction: "Put on your own oxygen mask first, before helping your child." To help their child take control of their emotions, parents should collaborate with them by asking them how they are feeling and helping them label their feelings. Parents should get down on the eye level of the child and explain that they are there to listen and help, not ridicule or threaten. For young children, parents can offer a well-loved stuffed animal or blanket to help the child recover.

Question

What can I do when the parents are doing their child's online homework?

Answer

Teachers need to have a conversation with parents to coach them on the importance of helping their child develop their emotional intelligence and take responsibility for their learning. Parents need to know teachers are on the same team and also want the best for their child. Teachers can explain that doing the child's homework is a disservice to the child because it takes the opportunity for learning away from the child. By being accessible to their child, parents can empower their child to make decisions about how and when to do their homework.

CHAPTER 7

Supporting Inclusivity
in Online Teaching

I maintain the same objectives for students with learning differences
but use (or create) different tracks of activities, depending upon students'
capabilities. I use online activities that allow them to make a variety of
choices. I let students know that I will read aloud directions and give
explanations as needed, but if they prefer to work independently, they
are welcome to do so.

—ALICE NICHOLS, educator

Online Learning Preference

Families have a variety of reasons for choosing to have their children attend virtual classes. Typically, they are seeking to provide them with an alternative education. They might be looking for flexibility, individualized support, a positive social environment, an appropriate level of challenge in material, or other factors in their educational environment.

Tonks and coauthors (2021) discovered parents enrolling their special education students in virtual classes "had left schools where they had experienced bullying, struggled academically, lacked adequate support, or did not receive legally mandated accommodations, and chose instead the online school because of its flexibility, teacher availability, and support" (183). Students who experience educational barriers when attending in-person schools may experience benefits in an online setting that they wouldn't otherwise (Murphy et al. 2019). No matter what the reason for their pursuit of online education, students will be affected in some way by their previous educational and life experiences.

Emotion- or Learning-Based Differences

What a student has experienced in their life—a life event or previous schooling situation—may have had a negative impact on their emotional state and emotional intelligence. Students with emotion- or learning-based differences may require specialized instruction or services according to their individualized education plans. Meeting those goals can be challenging, especially when there is a disagreement between stakeholders on how to best meet the student's educational needs. If their educational needs are not being met, students may react negatively to their schooling experience (Moore 2021).

To assist each student effectively throughout the course, teachers need to be aware of any learning disparities, but previous experiences may make parents and students reluctant to share learning differences or disabilities with the teacher or to ask for special accommodations. Teachers who create an inclusive, warm, and welcoming online environment help to promote a situation where families feel comfortable sharing sensitive information. As discussed in previous chapters, creating a welcoming learning environment by using inclusive behavior and language can support all learners, regardless of their previous experiences and individual challenges (Iqbal et al. 2021).

Each student carries with them their own challenges to online learning and may sometimes requires extra assistance to successfully learn online. Although not all students need special accommodations, having accommodations available and in place may benefit students in the virtual classroom. For example, students who have difficulty understanding what people say online may benefit from captioning webinar tools. Even with imperfect transcription, having the speaker's words shown on the screen during a webinar may help to relieve some of the tension that students could experience in the classroom. They no longer need to be concerned that they are missing information from the verbal interactions in the webinar because they can read along on the screen. This accommodation would be available to all students in the virtual classroom, not only to those who need it.

Accessible Learning Environment

Part of creating an accessible learning environment is to ensure that schools are caring communities that expand their mission to educate by filling in the gaps for families in need of assistance with teaching their children socializing skills. Fulfilling this daunting task can require teachers to go above and beyond their teaching duties and can benefit from the involvement of community members with schools. By providing a safe and accessible learning environment, teachers create opportunities to reach their students and promote their learning as well as their emotional intelligence (Bradley-Dorsey et al. 2022; Xiang et al. 2022).

When choosing the learning management system, webinar room, and other online applications, teachers and schools should consider accessibility. Course materials and applications should be compatible with assistive applications and technology, such as magnification tools, screen readers, voice recognition software, and other assistive third-party software.

Finding appropriate applications can be difficult, but being aware of the challenges students face can help teachers and schools choose applications that meet as many student needs as possible. Students with visual impairments may require additional assistance understanding what is being shown through the video feed if an educational system uses live video. Students with high social anxiety, those concerned with privacy issues, or those who are considered introverted, neurodiverse, and twice exceptional may not find it comfortable to be live on camera. Teachers and educational organizations should be mindful of individual student preferences, parental preferences, and safety issues when determining how to best align those preferences and issues with school policies.

Students might find it beneficial to use an accessibility tool in their home. Teachers can encourage their students to use the tool while completing schoolwork or while in the webinar. Accessibility tools may include screen readers, notetaking applications, work organizers, or talk-to-text applications.

Webinar Recordings

Webinar recordings may seem secondary to webinars themselves, but they are actually important tools for ensuring accessibility. To make the viewing experience more accessible, schools and organizations that make webinar recordings available may also provide written transcripts of the webinars. Sometimes copies of the recordings can be loaded into a third-party application that can automatically generate a written transcript of the recording.

Although some schools and organizations view recording webinars as optional, teachers are encouraged to record webinars whenever possible. Teachers should be cognizant, however, of privacy concerns when working with recordings of their students, especially if names and likenesses are included.

Despite privacy concerns, having a webinar recording available to students can ease student anxieties about missing important information. Students who are concerned that they missed, or can't remember, something crucial that was mentioned during the webinar can easily refer to the webinar recording. Recordings can also help students without a stable internet connection stay on top of the information presented in class.

Webinar recordings are particularly beneficial for students with learning differences. Students can return to the recording at any time to review it at their own pace. This is helpful if they struggle to keep up with the webinar, need to address confusion, or would like to take notes to solidify ideas in their minds.

To promote recordings' accessibility, recorded material should be high quality, easy to hear, easy to see, and easy to access. Teachers should review their recordings from time to time to ensure their system is operating correctly. They need to be sure the instructions for locating the recordings are clear, their cameras are focused, and their microphones pick up their voice clearly while eliminating background noise.

Most often, the LMS and webinar service will include a text-chat area. Students who have emerging typing skills may find it helpful to have their parent or another family member write their thoughts into the text-chat area. The typist can gradually retreat as the student's typing skills develop.

Accessibility in Instruction

One way to improve accessibility for students is to ensure that the instructions for assignments and projects are clear, detailed, and free of unfamiliar jargon. Using clear and accurate language does not mean that difficult or technical vocabulary and phrases should be avoided. On the contrary, use words that challenge students to learn and grow. Teachers should concentrate on using precise language to reach students more effectively.

Every time instructions are given to students, the teacher should go over them. Oftentimes, instructions seem clear when presented, but upon later review teachers may discover that the directions are confusing or unclear. During their review, teachers can also evaluate the accessibility and inclusivity of the material and make adjustments as necessary.

Information should be provided in a variety of formats to allow students to connect using their preferred learning method (Conklin and Dikkers 2021). For example, teachers can include instructions for an assignment through a text, a short video, an email message, and a webinar discussion. Determining how often and in what ways to express information is situational, but students often benefit from multiple reminders in multiple modalities.

Teachers may choose to provide additional instructions. When assigning a group project, the teacher might include clear instructions on how to communicate effectively with team members, how to choose a team leader, and how to divide tasks.

As teachers create the virtual classroom and design webinar information, they should make sure that their descriptions, headings, and labels are clear, consistent, and accessible. For instance, a teacher creating a virtual classroom should label the weeks in their course "Week 1, Week 2, and Week 3" rather than "Week 1, 2nd Week, and Week - 3." An inconsistent format is difficult to follow and may create undue stress for students, whereas information posted clearly and consistently creates continuity and familiarity, which may contribute to a sense of calm (Koh and Kan 2020).

Teachers should choose fonts that are clear and easy to read for all students, including those with dyslexia. Even if the teacher chooses to use more than one font, the fonts should all be discernible. Studies have shown that sans serif fonts are preferred when it comes to accessibility (Hojjati and Muniandy 2014; Rello and Baeza-Yates 2013). Additionally, larger font sizes may make the information easier to read (Rello et al. 2013). Some LMS and webinar systems allow the user to zoom in so the student can see the information on the screen more closely. Alternatively, a student or parent could take a screenshot or picture of the screen and use their computer or phone to zoom in.

When writing instructions or providing information, teachers should use inclusive language and avoid assumptions or stereotypes about disabilities, gender, race, and other characteristics. Representing diverse cultures, experiences, and perspectives in the imagery and language used in assignments, course materials, handouts, and presentations is critical to ensure a positive classroom culture. For example, a teacher may include a picture of a person holding a globe. Instead of choosing one that shows an adult's hands holding the globe, the teacher might opt to choose one of a student from a different culture holding the globe. By presenting their content through a different lens, the teacher is making sure as many students as possible are represented and a positive classroom culture is maintained.

All online visual information, especially in the virtual classroom, ought to include a description in an alternate text format or be brief and easy to understand. If a teacher is aware that a student has difficulty with their eyesight, they might verbally explain what the photos illustrate or provide the family with a description on the copy of their slides. Alternatively, parents can explain to their child what is seen on the screen, keeping in mind that this practice limits their child's autonomy.

Although prevalent across social media networks, abbreviations and acronyms may not always translate well to the virtual classroom. Abbreviations and acronyms may have more than one connotation, and the original meaning can be lost when taken out of context. To maintain clear communication and avoid confusion, any abbreviations, acronyms, idioms, and technical vocabulary should be clearly defined and explained. This can be especially important for students who are not native speakers of the language used in the course.

Fostering Open, Accessible Communication

To foster accessibility, different modes of communication—such as audio recording, email, messaging, text chat, and video recording—should be available to all students and their families. Students can benefit from specific tools like voice recordings, video recordings, and speech-to-text when communicating in class. Offering students a range of communication options might help them feel more at ease when sharing their ideas.

Teachers should encourage students to share any challenges or concerns they are experiencing so additional resources and assistance can be offered. Coaching students on how to communicate their concerns and questions can help them gain confidence in asking for help. Creating a system for parents and students to easily request accommodations in a confidential manner (between the teacher and the family) gives families an opportunity to feel supported (Dost et al. 2022).

> Accommodation is a key part of teaching and
> there are many ways to make this happen.
> —VALERIE FRANKEL, online educator

Making Accommodations

Flexibility and the capacity to modify the course to meet the needs of the student and their family can be advantageous to the child's emotional intelligence. Arguably, flexibility depends on emotional strength and the ability to remain comfortable with ambiguity when facing unexpected circumstances (Goleman 1998). Teachers, schools, and organizations should ensure assignments and assessments are accessible to all students by making accommodations that may involve the choice of learning materials, the time available for student work, and the amount and kind of student work required.

When creating the virtual classroom, teachers should use a variety of learning materials to accommodate different learning preferences and styles. The virtual classroom can include videos, audio recordings, online and offline learning games, audiobooks, printed materials such as books, large-print materials, PDFs, or websites with written information. Offering choice allows the student to select learning materials that align with their particular learning preferences and style.

A plethora of videos are available online from many different sources and creators, and they can be a useful learning tool for students, but they warrant special attention. Before including them in class, teachers should preview videos to be sure they contain accurate and up-to-date information that is appropriate for all of their students. Sometimes video creators include language or visuals that are inappropriate for some groups of students. Teachers must also be aware that videos with flashing or strobes might trigger a migraine or seizure in some children. If teachers are unable to find suitable videos, they may choose to create their own to share with their class.

Although some schools have time limits that are stricter than others, every effort should be made to give students ample time to complete their assignments. Accommodations should be made for students facing challenges to their learning or for those who are navigating unexpected situations beyond their control, but these accommodations need to be reasonable for both student and teacher. For example, if a writing course requires a student to complete an assignment going on to the next assignment, it would not be reasonable to enable a student to wait to turn in their paper at the end of the term. In the case of a homeschooled student, families can extend courses through the following semester or the summer, depending on the homeschooling laws in their area.

Alternative assignments or consideration for late submissions should be available for students who miss class for various reasons, such as doctor appointments, family travel, or a death in the family. Students with complex medical needs or students experiencing traumatic upheaval in their lives should be approached with understanding. If a student has health concerns that impede their ability to complete every single assignment, the teacher can work with the parent and student to make adjustments to the requirements. Instead of completing two writing prompts, the student may be assigned one. Instead of generating a written response to a prompt, the student may be asked to verbally explain their thoughts. Instead of watching several educational videos, the student may watch the one that supports the lesson the best.

Asynchronous activities, such as watching webinar recordings, can increase flexibility for students who are not able to attend the live webinars. This option allows students to complete the course when the live webinar schedule does not align with their schedule owing to various external factors, including prior commitments, overlapping medical appointments, and time zone differences.

Accommodation of student diversity can also be achieved by allowing students to choose their tasks or to modify them. Providing students with the capability to adjust the assignments while still meeting the learning objectives gives students the ability to tailor their learning experience to work best for them (Hawthorn-Embree et al. 2010).

Accommodation may also be required to cope with students' comfort level with group projects. Creating educational opportunities for students to interact and collaborate on projects may help students connect. However, not all students or families appreciate group work. Learning differences can get in the way of students making connections with each other. Furthermore, when all students in the group do not put forth the same amount of effort, some students may assume responsibility for more of the work, making it difficult for the teacher to ensure fairness.

> When you're teaching an online class it's vitally important to be flexible. Students and families have all kinds of things going on at home, and I've learned I need to be sensitive to that. These kids are doing amazing things, and whatever I can do to help them succeed at the things that are important to them is worth considering.
>
> —BECKY RIETHMEIER, classroom and online educator

Another accommodation to students' capacity in online learning is allowing for students to take a break when they are spending hours online attending live webinars and virtual school classes. Stretching, moving around in their chairs, standing up, walking around, and getting a snack can help students—and teachers—rejuvenate themselves and renew their focus on learning.

Teachers who make learning accommodations and modifications for their students in online classrooms can be viewed as simply good teachers who care. Caring teachers are concerned for the welfare of their individual students. They keep abreast of situational family crises and are prepared to offer their assistance. Teachers are not lowering their expectations and standards by offering accommodations or making modifications. Rather, they are responding to a problem or circumstance in ways that can be beneficial for the child.

See the table for questions that encourage teachers to reflect on their online teaching practices when thinking about accommodations and modifications.

Accommodations and Modifications

SELF-AWARENESS	SELF-MANAGEMENT	SOCIAL AWARENESS	RELATIONSHIP SKILLS	RESPONSIBLE DECISION-MAKING
How might I offer learning accommodations for my students, including those who are special needs, gifted, and twice exceptional?	How might I support students in completing assignments when they have extenuating circumstances, such as family emergencies?	How might I provide classroom breaks so students have time to develop relationships with their classmates?	How might I respond to student and parent feedback to demonstrate I am listening and care?	How might I remain flexible yet stick to the decisions I have made?

Challenges in Making Accommodations

Some online learning circumstances may accommodate learning differences more easily than others. Although accommodations may be legally required, a comprehensive online school in which students follow a graded track may not offer the flexibility of an online organization in which homeschooled students set their own schedules. Sometimes, accommodations cannot be made easily.

The LMS or webinar room may have technological limitations that prevent the class from meeting a student's needs. For example, an LMS platform may not use a dyslexia-friendly font that can meet the needs of a student with dyslexia. If the student is homeschooled and no change can be made to the LMS, the family can choose to enroll in a different online organization. If the student is enrolled in a public online school, however, the student may not be able to transfer to another school. If an alternative cannot be identified, a schoolwide change may need to be implemented. Unfortunately, a sitewide or schoolwide change may require time, which can exacerbate the student's difficulties. Knowing the limitations of the LMS, and informing families of them when relevant, can help alleviate issues.

Student Voices

Students want their voices to be heard. Giving them feedback forms to complete over the duration of the course will make them feel listened to and let teachers get to know them better. The form can ask how the student feels about the course accessibility and class inclusivity. Forms should also give students an opportunity to offer a self-assessment of their individual level of challenge.

Teachers need to be open and responsive to their students' comments and suggestions. It is not enough to simply listen to or read the feedback. Rather, after receiving and analyzing the feedback, teachers should use it to implement change or foster further positive results. This feedback can be a helpful tool for meeting each student's unique accessibility needs and making sure that the adjustments put in place are helping the student.

TEACHING TIP

Question

What can I do for my students who cannot look at the screen for long periods of time?

Answer

Students who get headaches from looking at the computer screen or have trouble maintaining eye contact with the screen need special accommodations in online classes. Parents and students should be encouraged to use adaptive technology; for instance, they could try changing the brightness or hue of the screen on their child's computer. Another idea is to send the student the presentation slides for the lesson before the webinar. That way, the presentation can be printed ahead of time so the student can follow along during the webinar with their computer screen off, using audio only.

CHAPTER 8

Recognizing the Challenges of Online Teaching

In my online classes, I emphasize the importance of fostering an environment
that is harmonious and conducive to collaboration. Establishing clear and
upfront guidelines for respectful communication forms the foundation of this
environment, serving as the fundamental basis for interactions among students
in discussion forums, live sessions, or group activities. With careful
monitoring of these interactive spaces, I promptly identify
and address any conflicts that may arise.

— JESSICA KOEHLER, PhD, online educator

The Extra Demands of Online Teaching

Online teaching has a host of benefits, which range from flexibility in scheduling
to connections with a global audience. But online teaching comes with its own
challenges that aren't present when teaching in person. Some, like simple technology issues, are easily fixed, while others, like meeting every student's educational needs, are more difficult. The goal, of course, is for teachers to meet as
many of the virtual classroom challenges as possible while making sure that their
own mental health is not compromised.

Unfortunately, school administrators often expect teachers to do work far
beyond their everyday duties and contractual scope (Farmer 2020; Jacobs and
Teise 2019). Besides fulfilling and exceling at their educational responsibilities,
teachers are expected to meet the emotional needs of their students by being
aware of each student's state of mind, putting a plan in place to help each student,

and taking the actions necessary to carry out each plan (Farmer 2020). In addition, knowing that students do better when issues and problems can be quickly addressed in real time, teachers may feel the added stress of time sensitivity (Santi et al. 2022). The pressure teachers feel to meet and exceed expectations can be overwhelming and exhausting.

These professional expectations can significantly impact teachers' perceptions of their working conditions and their level of satisfaction in their profession. Teachers with a more positive working environment tend to report higher satisfaction with teaching (Boyd et al. 2011). Therefore, the goal when creating a virtual classroom is to make it an environment where students and teachers thrive— where the emotional intelligence of the student *and* the teacher is supported.

Engaging Students

First and foremost, to foster student engagement, teachers and students need reliable technology. Dependable equipment and Wi-Fi access are critical for a positive and productive online learning experience, while unreliable technology can cause stress and frustration for both teachers and students. For many school districts, the lack of availability of up-to-date computers is an issue. Furthermore, lack of equal access to technology greatly impacts children who come from economically disadvantaged backgrounds, creating a significant learning gap between these students and those who come from privileged backgrounds.

Next, because active learning can be harder to discern in a virtual classroom, teachers need to be aware of and stay committed to student engagement. They need to design activities that engage students in using information to achieve a learning outcome with a specific point in mind (Kosslyn 2021). Online teachers will find that talking and interacting are more engaging for students than lecturing and should design their material accordingly.

Students are more attentive if teachers talk in small blocks of time, with frequent checks for understanding or breaks for hands-on involvement (Lumpkin 2021). Young children, who especially benefit from structure and routine, need to actively participate in webinars because they can become easily distracted online. It is not uncommon for a young student to log into the classroom, become disinterested, and move to another room or browser window, not to return until the end of class.

Teachers should provide a structured classroom that uses a range of collaborative tools and methods to keep students involved. Since not all students have the same learning style, teachers need to offer activities that address kinesthetic, auditory, and visual learning. When students are learning through fun activities, they are often more motivated to become involved. The integration of riddles, games, and problem-solving challenges with online lessons can increase students' motivation and promote a love of learning (Kerrigan and Aghekyan 2022).

It can be demanding for teachers to keep track of every student online, especially in a course with many students. Teachers may find it helpful to record their students' participation and understanding through the use of a simple tally. In this way, they can easily see which students are not participating in class or need additional help. Teachers can also access and replay classroom recordings to check on students' participation or to revisit any questions or problems that arose during a particular class. With this valuable information, teachers can address any learning concerns when preparing for their next class.

In addition to checking on student participation and understanding of content, teachers can fine-tune and adjust the pacing of their online lessons once they determine how well students are managing assignments. This information on student progress informs teachers about their teaching practices in a virtual environment and encourages them to reflect and make changes that better meet their students' needs. Integrating input from students helps to create a student-centered environment—a personalized setting in which students can improve their emotional intelligence and know they have a voice that is being heard—where students can become invested in their own education.

Teacher Self-Advocacy

The culture of a school or learning community doesn't always lend itself to teacher self-advocacy. The level of support teachers receive varies from institution to institution and can deeply impact a teacher's efficacy and emotions associated with their classrooms. These emotions can be compounded when teachers work to develop a virtual classroom that fosters students' emotional intelligence. Teachers who receive emotional intelligence training may, in addition to recognizing their own emotions and those of their students, learn how to navigate difficulties and communicate empathically in ways that allow them to both advocate for themselves and help children build their emotional intelligence (Merry 2021). Outside of the virtual classroom, teachers may feel pressure from the parents of their students. Parents may have high expectations, including wanting the teacher to help them address their child's mental health challenges. These and similar expectations may leave the teacher feeling overwhelmed, especially if there is a mismatch between actual or perceived expectations and the teacher's actual or perceived ability to handle the situation (Ekornes 2017). In cases where teachers feel unsupported or overloaded with responsibilities, they need to advocate for themselves to ensure their work benefits both their students and themselves.

Online teaching requires unique skills and preparation. If a teacher is moving from an in-person classroom to a virtual classroom for the first time and doesn't have the background knowledge to teach effectively online, they will need more support to succeed, especially if they are not volunteering to teach online (Barbour and Unger 2014). Online schools and organizations should provide teachers with ongoing support to help them meet their students' educational needs (Dolighan and Owen 2021). If they aren't receiving the support they need, teachers' emotional intelligence may suffer and they may not be effective in the virtual classroom (Mérida-López et al. 2020).

One study "showed significant associations between support from colleagues and supervisors with teacher engagement and intention to quit . . . suggesting that the perception of supportive relations with colleagues and supervisors was significantly associated with work engagement, which, in turn, was linked with lower withdrawal intention" (Mérida-López et al. 2020, 148). The researchers added that the "teachers with the lowest levels of work engagement reported low support from colleagues or supervisors, together with low emotional intelligence.

Similarly, highest intentions to quit were reported by those teachers reporting low work engagement and low emotional intelligence" (141). The team suggested that educational administrators should "pay attention to EI [emotional intelligence] levels when designing programs to promote teachers' work motivation and commitment" (148).

If no efforts are made to encourage teachers and they do not feel supported, teachers need to be proactive and advocate for themselves, just as they would for their students. They need to seek assistance from other teachers within the organization or reach out to administration staff to find solutions.

In some cases, difficult situations are persistent and a solution cannot readily be found. Teachers facing seemingly insurmountable issues may benefit from joining professional learning communities where teachers can discuss issues and get advice from others in similar situations (Turner and Brannon 2022). Many professional learning communities can be found on social media. Through online groups and support organizations, teachers can gain the support they need and nurture relationships with others in similar situations. By making sure their emotional intelligence needs are being met, teachers can turn to help their fellow teachers in need and their students, including by providing support for their students' emotional intelligence.

Teacher Advocacy for Students

Teachers set the tone for the virtual classroom early on by modeling the types of behaviors they want from their students and establishing the framework for the virtual classroom culture. Throughout their time together, the teacher may learn more about their students, especially as emotions are communicated (Duzgun 2022). As students share more with teachers, teachers may discover behaviors or events that may need to be addressed.

With any situation involving students, schools and educational organizations may have protocols in place, and these protocols should be followed, especially when dealing with serious issues such as cyberbullying or inappropriate behavior. Teachers who work independently should create protocols to address situations that warrant intervention. Protocols can range from simple (what to do when the internet connection is lost during a webinar) to complex (what to do when a student discusses self-harm). As with any challenging situation that arises in teaching, the response will be individualized and specific to the situation. However, having a general protocol in place may help minimize stress.

Regardless of whether a teacher is affiliated with a school or works independently, it falls upon the teacher to advocate for what is best for the student's educational, physical, or emotional well-being. During these times, the focus should be on caring authentically about the whole student, taking into account what is happening in their lives, in class, outside of class, in their homes, and within their communities (Rolón-Dow 2005).

Although all avenues should be explored, advocating for a student might even mean suggesting that online education may not be appropriate for the learner. Some students may benefit more from in-person education (Ruecker 2021). Of course, the teacher can only make suggestions, which may not align with a student's final placement.

Student Interpersonal Issues

When Howard Gardner published the *Theory of Multiple Intelligences* in 1983, he initially focused on seven intelligences, though more were added in succeeding years. The *Theory of Multiple Intelligences* has offered numerous approaches that have proven to be instrumental in school improvement initiatives around the world (Chen et al. 2009). Moreover, two of the original personal intelligences—interpersonal and intrapersonal—have been shown to be particularly useful in recognizing and managing one's emotions.

Teachers who have established a virtual classroom culture and friendly environment may come across students who are struggling with interpersonal issues. Problems that seem small to adults can often seem large and overwhelming to children. Having an empathetic adult in their lives to help them through challenges has a positive impact on students' ability to problem-solve in the future (Westerberg et al. 2020).

Exposure to Different Social and Cultural Contexts

Thinking and learning are not carried out in a vacuum but rather in a social and a cultural context. A student's emotional intelligence is impacted by their family's culture and their own identity (Fischer and Bidell 2006). Past social experiences, reputation, and cultural history impact how individuals make decisions. Some students may find it difficult to relate to each other owing to these cultural differences.

Furthermore, in virtual classes, unlike in a neighborhood brick-and-mortar school, students may live on opposite sides of the world. They may encounter classmates from different socioeconomic, religious, ethnic, and racial backgrounds. For students who are not used to relating to others from different backgrounds, this cross-cultural engagement might be difficult. It is crucial, however, that students learn to work with individuals from varying and diverse backgrounds to achieve a cohesive class culture.

Teachers can use various ways of helping students relate to others from different backgrounds. Digital storytelling may help students raise their awareness and improve their emotional intelligence when relating to others. As teachers look for ways to connect with their students, and ways to connect students with their peers, Muhammad (2020) recommends that teachers focus on four main areas:

- developing students' identities, such as the role they play on the planet,
- developing students' skills, such as questioning a source of information,
- developing intellectualism about topics from around the world, such as gathering facts and then applying that knowledge in a meaningful way, and
- developing critical thinking skills by asking questions and analyzing works.

Teachers can also add an element of joy, such as giving students the chance to choose what assignment to complete or making a connection to students' families by having them reflect on a topic discussed in class at home. The class can then come together to share their individual discussions to find commonality and celebrate differences (Muhammad et al. 2021).

Challenges with Group Work

Employers increasingly view skills such as problem-solving, communication, collaboration, interpersonal skills, social skills, and time management as essential when they hire individuals for team environments. As a consequence, schools may require students to learn these skills by working on projects in groups.

A 2001 study revealed a compelling relationship between students' emotional intelligence and team harmony—their ability to work effectively together with positive interdependence and interaction. The successful team demonstrated characteristics of emotional intelligence that supported their collaboration and, subsequently, their achievement. On the other hand, the dysfunctional team exhibited negative interdependence, poor communication, and lack of consideration, empathy, and understanding (Luca and Tarricone 2001).

Ideally, when a teacher organizes students into groups to work together on a cooperative project, the students would work together effectively on the assignment. They would harmoniously determine the group roles, create a plan, and put that plan into action. Unfortunately, the ideal doesn't always happen. Although students may begin their work on a positive note and get off to a good start, sometimes situations go awry. One student may be left to complete the task for the group, or one student might disregard others' opinions and take over the project completely. Other times, the entire process may fizzle out, leaving the group with the shell of a project or a missed deadline. Students in these group situations can become stressed, and their emotional intelligence can be negatively impacted. Instead of being a fun, developmental, transformative experience, the project can become just the opposite, leading students to dread working with others.

Working in groups online may present itself differently than working with an in-person group. Although personality conflicts and failure by some group members to complete their required tasks may arise in both in-person and virtual environments, those issues may be compounded online. Students in a group that already spends hours together online may benefit from that time, compared with students who attend webinars together only once a week.

When group members don't have time allotted to meet during the regularly scheduled webinars, they may need assistance scheduling meetings and learning how to communicate with the group effectively. Before group work begins, teachers should set up a space in their virtual classroom with pointers on how to effectively work in a group, such as reminders about what to do if a conflict arises. These reminders should be included even if the same information is covered in a webinar so students can easily reference the information in case an issue arises.

Helping Students Communicate in Group Work

If group members do not know each other well before working together, teachers may want to include simple getting-to-know-you activities that highlight group work. In addition, teachers may include ideas about how students can effectively communicate with each other—not only the intricacies of effective communication but also the method they use to communicate. The mode of communication (e.g., email, messages in the learning management system) will depend on the age and maturity level of the students.

Teachers should urge that students and parents sign a contract reminding students of their obligations and stressing that parents are accountable for their children's behavior outside of the virtual classroom if students are using a platform without adult supervision. Parents should be copied on correspondence between younger students, while older students may be responsible for communicating with each other on their own.

Teachers ought to set up a system where students report back with updates on the project's progress at regular intervals. The timeline of check-ins can be adjusted to adequately address the complexity and length of the project. For example, if the project is due in a month, students can check in with the teacher once or twice a week. Students may want to specify a group member who will communicate with the teacher, but all group members should be included in correspondence with the teacher so everyone is on the same page. To identify problems early, teachers may choose to add brief questionnaires that groups or individual members fill out on a regular basis.

Teachers may also choose to be included in the correspondence so they can help guide students toward the goal. Whenever appropriate, providing students with autonomy over their work is advisable. Students need the opportunity to work with others without direct adult oversight so they can practice life skills in a safe, supportive, learning environment. However, having access to the group's communication can help teachers discover the root of a problem or stop an issue before it occurs.

Although many issues can arise when students are working together, there are a few particularly common stressful scenarios:

- A diligent student takes on the responsibility of the project for the group.
- A struggling student isn't able to keep up with the group.
- A conflict arises within the group.

Thinking about potential courses of action in these situations will help the teacher prepare in advance. No matter the situation, it is important to identify the root cause of the problem, reframe the event into a learning experience, and proceed from there.

When a diligent student takes on responsibility for the group's project, it is either because students in the group are not participating or because their ideas have been overpowered. To prevent either situation, the teacher should begin the group work activity with instructions on how to choose a group leader, how to assign roles to the members of the group, and how to make sure that each group member's voice is heard and valued. To ensure that students know what is expected of them and can carry it out, teachers must communicate clear and organized expectations.

If the diligent student has already taken over, the teacher should determine if it was because the other team members' voices were being drowned out or because they were not speaking up. This is easier to determine, of course, if the teacher is included in the correspondence. Teachers can instruct the group to assign each student a section on the group's graphic organizer with their contribution to the daily conversation. This information can then be shared with the teacher. The completed form, showing the ideas and engagement of every student, is also a useful tool for self-reflection for teachers so they can consider what is needed to support their students.

Being included in correspondence with team members will also help teachers determine whether a student is struggling to keep up with their part of the project. If a student is having trouble keeping up, the teacher may intervene and suggest a different approach. When a course is part of a school district, certain general criteria for assignments may need to be met. If the class is separate from a district, however, more alternatives are available. A teacher could suggest changing the nature of the assignment, such as moving from a video production to a slideshow presentation, or changing the scope of the project to a less ambitious one.

Handling Conflict in Group Work

Conflict can occur within groups and in fact is often unavoidable. It usually arises when group members do not share a common vision and hold a difference of opinion. When the stakes are high, students' emotions run deep. Group members need a high degree of emotional intelligence to treat their colleagues with trust, respect, and connection. It is important to be able to effectively handle conflict by getting one's needs met without passivity or aggression. For students, it can be useful to practice the skills of questioning, seeking clarification, saying "and" instead of "but," and offering solutions to defend one's position and remain proactive (Bradberry 2023).

When conflict arises, students can experience elevated stress levels. Emotions that run rampant can even cause physical symptoms, such as headaches. Teachers need to intervene with communication that helps students address the struggle and solve the issues promptly. Providing students with a plan on how to handle conflict in a group setting can prepare them for what to do in an actual life situation. It is important for students to know that to understand the ideas their group members contribute, they must be open-minded and respect the dynamics of the group. As they address arguments or differences of opinion, group members must be receptive to creative alternatives. Students should also be encouraged to reach out to the teacher on their own in the case of conflict and seek the teacher's help if the conflict is not resolved quickly.

> When students are struggling with interpersonal conflicts, it is important to set the ground rules from the start, such as calm voices and no interruptions. Students need to understand I am not taking sides—I am an impartial "judge" who can help them problem-solve together.
> —KAREN ARNSTEIN, PhD, online educator

Student Intrapersonal Issues

A range of students' intrapersonal issues can affect their learning and pose challenges for teachers. Oftentimes, traditionally run schools require students to complete and submit specific assignments to prove mastery of a concept. Unfortunately, not every assessment is geared toward every student. Online teachers can often be creative with the assignments and modes of learning, especially for optional assignments. Teachers should collaborate creatively with students to decide which assignments and platforms can help them demonstrate mastery of the educational material in a way that fosters positive emotional intelligence. Sometimes it takes collaboration, creativity, and patience to get to the point where the student can appropriately show they know the material while finding the joy in the process of learning.

Student learning levels may vary from student to student even in the same class. The early warning indicators that a student is struggling may go unnoticed, so it is a good idea for teachers to check in with their students informally or formally to ask "Are you feeling challenged?" Students should be experiencing enough challenges in their education to stay interested and to learn without feeling overwhelmed. Students' answers to this question will help the teacher—and the student—fine-tune the student's learning.

Engagement and participation vary from student to student. Acuña and Blacklock (2022) discovered that most of the off-task or defiant behaviors students exhibit relate to their refusal to complete assignments. Teachers may improve the odds of reaching their students, keeping students engaged, and helping them learn by getting to know their students and creating an academic culture conducive to learning. Even when discussing, for example, an accusation of plagiarism with a student, teachers need to be transparent yet connect emotionally to make a meaningful impact.

Although teachers may want to tailor their lessons to each student individually, doing so can be difficult if they aren't able to work one on one with each student. This raises the question: how does a teacher reach as many students as possible when teaching to a group?

In response to this question, some argue that teachers need to motivate students by supporting their students' autonomy and competence. Others say that teachers should adopt demotivating behaviors, like backing away from students and keeping their distance. One study of college students determined that because students respond differently to the way teachers behave, "to foster positive student engagement in virtual classrooms, teachers should use the right blend of motivating and demotivating teaching behaviors" (Gupta 2023, 130). Another study found that student engagement depends significantly on the teacher's teaching style, their timeliness in providing feedback and responding to student inquiries, and the caliber of the content delivered during their time with the students (Dwivedi et al. 2019). Overall, however, there must be a balance between assisting students and giving them space to learn and grow on their own. Consideration should also be given to the students' ages, ability levels, and background knowledge.

Resistance to Completing Assignments

When a student is not engaged and becomes resistant to completing assignments, there might be a number of reasons, including antipathy toward a particular assignment or topic, or an overarching external cause. Teachers may need to be creative in their approach to help students who exhibit signs of resistance.

It's crucial for teachers to keep in mind that the solution they come up with for a problem should work well with the remainder of the course. If the coursework must be completed in a certain way, teachers should remember to stress to students that this is an opportunity to practice completing work that might not be exciting or deeply purposeful. However, those less exciting assignments should be limited, and those offering flexibility should be more numerous.

A teacher might come up with a solution to these situations on their own or involve the student and their parents. Bringing the student into the discussion can help foster student self-efficacy. In a meeting, email, or similar communication, the teacher can share thoughts about how to adjust an assignment or suggest the student attend designated office hours for extra help. The teacher can encourage the student and parent to offer additional solutions or ask the family to provide additional context to the situation.

Issues on the World Wide Web

Adults need to be diligent in protecting children online. Teachers should regularly review the course material before sharing information, especially internet links, with students. Because the internet is constantly evolving, a website that is appropriate at one time might be inappropriate the next time it is accessed.

The virtual classroom and the webinar room that teachers create should be safe for students. Since the online world beyond the virtual walls can be unpredictable, teachers are urged to remind parents to be vigilant about what their child is doing online to make sure they are being responsible. Teachers may want to share information about effective parental controls, phone alerts, and other tools while remembering that it is important to foster student privacy, self-reliance, and responsibility.

When students work outside of the learning management system or similar platforms—browsing a website, watching a video, or surfing the internet—they are likely to encounter at least one online advertisement. Online ads can be highly distracting to students. If students have not been exposed to many advertisements, teachers should share information about how to respond to online ads with both students and parents. For example, teachers can explain to parents how to disable pop-up ads, use parental controls, and spot advertisements when searching online. In this way, both students and parents can begin to recognize and ignore websites that target them with advertisements.

Privacy Concerns

Student online safety, including identity protection, is one aspect of online learning that must be addressed. A major challenge is to ensure that individuals are protected while they are sharing information with others online. First and foremost, parents should always be involved whenever and wherever there is a question about student safety. If an educational system does not have a plan in place or the teacher is operating on their own, the teacher should provide parents with forms that address safety concerns. They should also outline their own safety protocols, including the steps they will take to ensure students are protected. Teachers, or the educational organization, should ensure documents are signed by both parents and students where applicable.

Teachers should remember to be cognizant of their own safety as well. They ought to keep copies of all correspondence, including emailed summaries of phone conversations that cannot be recorded. Additionally, teachers need to record every moment in a webinar where students are present. This practice allows students to return to the webinar recording to review material and allows teachers to review any situations that arose in a webinar.

TEACHING TIP

Question

*What can I do when a student fails
to turn in an online assignment?*

Answer

When a student doesn't turn in an online assignment, the teacher needs to pause and view it as a teachable moment. To turn things around, the teacher can meet with the student in a chat room or after class to show concern by listening to what is going on in the student's life. Failure to hand in an assignment should be seen as an opportunity to make adjustments or offer choices to help the student succeed.

CHAPTER 9

Empowering Emotional Intelligence in Today's Virtual Classroom

I am always on the lookout for students using fixed mindset language and work to reframe it with growth mindset verbiage. For example, a student in Chemistry class who did not have a Calculus background was feeling inadequate and unable to respond to a question. I assured the student that they were capable of approaching the question with the math concepts they already had. Then I presented some guiding questions to help work through the problem. I reinforced the good work that was done and the value of the process.

—KATIE KOESSLER, online educator

Adapting to a New Norm

The COVID-19 pandemic changed the way we educate children forever. Teachers perceived the pandemic as influencing what they taught, how they taught, and the roles and relationships between teachers, parents, and students (Brigandi et al. 2022). Because in-person opportunities were limited or nonexistent during that time, many teachers and students experienced a lack of interpersonal relationships (Pešikan et al. 2021). This was especially true for teachers and students who were new to hybrid or virtual learning. Many teachers teaching virtually for the first time found it difficult to connect with students online. Many also found it challenging to acquire and become proficient in appropriate strategies and tools to communicate with students and their families in an online setting. To maintain interest, enthusiasm, and commitment in a community of virtual learners that relied on technology, teachers needed to establish a connection with their students and their students' families that demonstrated their online presence.

When millions of classes transitioned to online settings because of the pandemic, those who were not used to online learning discovered it was time to rethink education. Virtual teaching and learning would require an open mind, determination, and a willingness to struggle. Teachers set out on a path to learn new software programs, create online resources, and build relationships with students in a virtual environment. Acquiring new knowledge involves a learning curve that does not happen in isolation. Teachers and students new to online learning engaged in the struggle to make sense of the learning process. They developed new skills and acquired a new understanding of the need to incorporate values, ideas, and emotions—the human element.

As schools slowly navigated away from the distance-learning restrictions imposed by the pandemic, many districts resumed in-person classrooms or moved toward a hybrid or virtual setting. It became a huge task to rebuild the school community and social support systems for both students and teachers (Posamentier 2021). School districts began to recognize the value of social and emotional learning and soon connected emotional intelligence to the classroom curriculum as a way for students to process their emotions.

Teachers are the engine that drives social and emotional learning in classrooms. Warm teacher-child relationships support deep learning and promote positive social-emotional development among students, while poorly managed social and emotional demands by teachers negatively impact the academic achievement and behavior of students (Schonert-Reichl 2017). Students who master social and emotional learning skills get along better with others, have more academic and professional success, and experience better mental and physical health as adults (Jones et al. 2017).

Before they could help students understand and manage their emotions, it became imperative for teachers to deal first with their own emotions and stress.

Teachers also had to develop new habits of thinking, using fresh strategies and tools to deepen their knowledge of how to best help their students online.

Interruption of Learning

The pandemic interrupted instruction in many ways, requiring teachers to constantly catch up while facing unprecedented challenges. Teachers addressed academic gaps and diverse learning needs in their classrooms, as they remained mindful of the most vulnerable groups—Black, Latino, and homeless students—while revising lesson plans to help absentee students get back on track (Esquivel 2022).

Learning losses were substantial, especially for those who were at risk of losing the protection that school-based learning offered to their well-being and lifelong opportunities. The restrictions on social interaction resulted in a variety of shortfalls, including a lack of extracurricular activities, cancellation of exams for future acceptance at schools, and lack of sanitary facilities and free school meals. Minimal social, emotional, or psychological support was available due to shifts in programming (Holmes 2020).

Interpreting Emotions

In an in-person classroom, teachers experience daily face-to-face situations that enable them to get to know and understand their students and, by addressing the individual and personal needs of each student, ensure the comfort and safety of the classroom environment. Through this observation and direct interaction, teachers are able to cultivate relationships with students while supporting their academic and social-emotional growth. This is not done as easily in a virtual classroom.

In online settings as well as in person, paying close attention to body language is important in communication. An individual's body language can be used to interpret and decipher their intents and feelings at a given moment (Tipper et al. 2015). As previously discussed, it is vital to observe *all* signals—facial expressions, gestures, eye gaze, posture, and personal distance—and not just one isolated expression (Cherry 2023). By observing this nonverbal communication, online teachers can develop emotional intelligence and foster the skill of understanding their students' feelings and moods.

Emotions, feelings, and thoughts can take hundreds of forms and in turn produce a wide range of actions (Goleman 1995). Therefore, teachers need to be careful to appropriately read the emotions expressed by their students and avoid assuming they understand how their students are feeling. To better identify and understand a student's emotions, online teachers should ask questions to clarify a situation and listen carefully to the student's response.

The acronym STANCE, meaning "staying tender and nurturing compassionate experiences," was created by Ekman (1992) to foster compassion while addressing challenging emotions. Online teachers need to listen to students with an open mind and make sure their personal feelings don't affect or interfere with what they are saying, being conscious of their own nonverbal cues. A good technique for letting a student know they are being heard is to repeat what has been said in the student's own words.

Although it may not be possible to personally speak with a student who is having a difficult day and intervene before it escalates, online teachers can meet with students in a virtual classroom later on or go to a private chat room to talk. In this way, online teachers can adapt their teaching to meet the emotional needs of their students, allowing them to concentrate and refocus on their learning.

Emotional Distancing in Students

Online teachers should be concerned if their students appear to be emotionally disconnected in the classroom. Negative emotions have an adverse effect on learning (Wortha et al. 2019), so it is critical for online teachers to identify and recognize instances of significant negativity.

In one study, undergraduate students enrolled in online courses participated in a survey on the growth of emotional intelligence during the learning process. Although limited in scope, the study found that most students thought virtual learning made it easier to share and transmit information, but it did not signifi-cantly enhance emotional intelligence. Even though they supported virtual edu-cation, the majority expressed feeling alone. They thought virtual education lacked social connections and relationship-building opportunities, as well as di-minishing attention, interaction, and recognition from their teachers (Babu and Koduru 2022). Such feelings of loneliness may have been fostered by a lack of a sense of community, which can negatively affect online learning experiences.

It is critical therefore that teachers understand how their online presence and attitude affect the mindset and behavior of their students. Online teachers themselves must be emotionally prepared before they can succeed in bringing emotional intelligence to their virtual classrooms. Through reflection and self-assessment, teachers can make informed decisions about how to invest their time and energy into teaching virtually.

Acquiring a Growth Mindset
and an Optimistic Attitude

Teachers must have a positive attitude about their role as online instructors. De-veloping a growth mindset about teaching and learning in a virtual environment is one way to do this. A growth mindset is "based on the belief that your basic qualities are things you can cultivate through your efforts" (Dweck 2006, 7). By modeling a growth mindset in class, online teachers can influence students to develop their own growth mindset. This mindset is not about achieving immedi-ate perfection; it is about learning over time and making progress by confronting a challenge (Dweck 2007).

Teachers and students can also make a personal choice to adopt an attitude of optimism. Optimism can be perceived as a personal belief that one's thoughts and actions can be positive, favorable, and desirable stimuli in an ever-changing world. Optimism, in addition to enthusiasm, self-confidence, and clarity of vision, can help inspire people to keep moving forward (Fullan 2001).

Goleman (1998) also views optimism as a great motivator. Despite setbacks and frustrations, "optimism is an attitude that buffers people against falling into apathy, hopelessness, or depression in the face of tough going" (Goleman 1995, 79). In this way, optimism can likely help lower stress and lessen feelings of helplessness. When teachers demonstrate a growth mindset and optimism and instill these qualities in their students, they help students develop and improve their academic abilities and promote their emotional intelligence.

Fostering a Growth Mindset

SELF-AWARENESS	SELF-MANAGEMENT	SOCIAL AWARENESS	RELATIONSHIP SKILLS	RESPONSIBLE DECISION-MAKING
How might I facilitate goal setting in my classroom?	How might I model a growth mindset in my online classroom?	How might I encourage effort and perseverance in my students' performance?	How might I empower students to acknowledge and celebrate their own and others' growth?	How can I help students accept responsibility for their errors in a way that fosters learning?

Teaching for Emotional Learning

There are many valuable tools teachers can use to guide them in creating curriculum and planning lessons that lead to emotional learning. One is the TIEL (teaching for intellectual and emotional learning) model of curricular design. TIEL helps teachers develop students' thinking skills in addition to qualities of character. It offers a color-coded wheel that graphically depicts character qualities and thinking operations to help teach students responsibility, compassion, and self-direction. This model focuses on developing five qualities of character (appreciation, mastery, ethical reasoning, empathy, and reflection) as well as five thinking operations (cognition, memory, evaluation, convergent thinking, and divergent thinking) (Folsom 2009). By learning about various areas of the wheel and making connections between them, TIEL teachers can become aware of strategies for teaching intellectual and emotional thinking that bring about success.

A second guide for teaching emotional thinking and learning strategies is the CASEL framework from the Collaborative for Academic, Social, and Emotional Learning (2023). CASEL promotes social and emotional learning by supporting empathy, resilience, and relationship building.

Similar to TIEL, CASEL uses a graphic wheel to illustrate attributes that online learners require, especially since COVID-19. At the center of the CASEL wheel are five core social and emotional competencies to support learning and development: self-awareness, self-management, social awareness, responsible decision-making, and relationship-building skills. Radiating from the center are four key settings where students live and grow: classrooms, schools, families and caregivers, and communities. Importantly, school-family-community partnerships coordinate and create equitable learning environments across all of these contexts.

The goal of both the CASEL and TIEL models is to support students in developing their interpersonal and intrapersonal awareness. Both models have the capacity to lead to academic success, fulfilling careers, and good mental health and wellness.

Individuals who hold a growth mindset look for ways they can improve and develop their emotional intelligence. The Yale Center for Emotional Intelligence (2022), a research center in New Haven, Connecticut, affirms that emotions drive learning, decision-making, creativity, relationships, and health and teaches people how to develop their emotional intelligence, using an evidence-based approach.

The Yale Center offers a five-step systematic program called RULER for integrating emotional intelligence in the classroom. RULER stands for five skills: recognizing, understanding, labeling, expressing, and regulating. RULER builds an awareness of the feelings children experience and provides them with a positive way to express these feelings. It boasts a proven success record in demonstrating that emotional intelligence improves outcomes for leaders, educators, and students in schools serving students in grades pre-K–12.

When classes made use of RULER, as students became more focused and the classroom climate improved, students and teachers formed better relationships and teachers experienced less burnout. Children were less anxious and depressed; they achieved better academic success in addition to exhibiting greater social skills and fewer behavioral issues like bullying (Brackett and Rivers 2014a).

When teachers are stressed, students in their classes are also stressed and exhibit worse academic performance and increased behavioral problems (Wood 2017). However, the positive results demonstrated by RULER have important implications for the mental health of teachers and students when managing negative emotions. It is imperative to provide emotional support to alleviate any adverse effects of negativity for the well-being of both teachers and students in virtual classrooms.

Emotional Intelligence Habits

Emotional intelligence can be broken down into two parts: (1) personal competence, consisting of self-awareness and self-management, and (2) social competence, consisting of awareness and understanding of other people's moods, behaviors, and motives as elements in improving relationships. Forming good personal and social competence habits and breaking bad ones can increase emotional intelligence, which is vital for personal success and fulfillment. Listening and observing, for example, are key to social awareness. By regulating anger in times of conflict, individuals can become more skillful in managing relationships, which are an essential and fulfilling part of life (Bradberry 2023).

Connecting Emotional Intelligence to Online Teaching

As previously stated, the need to teach emotional intelligence and the importance of emotional connectivity in virtual learning are not new concepts. Like all teachers, those who teach online have the opportunity to improve a child's educational experience by building relationships based on positive interpersonal connections. Research reveals that students who had a caring relationship with teachers had an increased desire to learn and stronger confidence in their abilities

(Pappas 2015). Students who experienced stronger affiliations with teachers were more engaged and performed better in school (Rio Poncela et al. 2021). Students' development of relationships with teachers and peers is critical to learning.

To improve communication skills and build genuine connections that foster relationships in virtual classrooms, online teachers need to help students develop their personal and social competencies. Chapter 1 revealed the five areas of competency: self-awareness, self-regulation, motivation, empathy, and social skills (Goleman 1998). Since emotions can be triggered by many factors and may elicit numerous reactions, they can often be difficult for online teachers to identify in a virtual environment. Unless the teacher is intentionally conscious of monitoring a child's personal and social competencies, emotions and reactions can go unnoticed, which can impact the child's academic and social-emotional development.

Because emotional intelligence is as important as cognitive ability, students who are taught to recognize and manage their emotions are more focused in school (William Woods University 2021). A lack of student focus and productivity can impact a student's ability to develop classroom relationships (Pešikan et al. 2021; Darwish 2021) and interfere with learning.

Furthermore, the home environment can be distracting for students and interfere with their activity and productivity in a virtual class (Turner and Brannon 2022). This is especially true for families who are not used to virtual learning. Parents of students new to virtual learning may experience a learning curve as they adapt to their role supporting their child's education at home. Parents must ensure that their children log into classes and are actively involved in virtual learning (Dost et al. 2022). Unfortunately, parents are often unaware of the accommodations needed to help their child succeed in online learning. Teachers can advise parents to ensure students have the opportunity to succeed.

Supporting Emotional Intelligence in the Online Classroom

The development of emotional intelligence is a critical component of education. Rather than considering it an add-on to the curriculum, teachers need to include it in daily lesson plans and teachable moments that happen in their classrooms.

There are many ways for teachers to support emotional intelligence in their classrooms. An introductory scavenger hunt is a fun way to encourage students to explore the software program and locate various curriculum and resource areas in the course. During instruction, teachers can employ various techniques, such as providing clear directions and deadlines, offering opportunities for students to work both individually and in small flexible groups, and motivating students with interest and inquiry-based learning. Teachers need to step away from the lecture mode, with its requirements for rote learning, to become coaches or facilitators of knowledge.

Teachers can provide students with choices in terms of process, product, and content to promote students' decision-making. Choices encourage students to develop empathy and leadership skills by reflecting on and considering others' perspectives. One way to engage online students is through journaling, which can be adapted to the student's learning style. Students can take notes in a diary, a log book, or a desktop folder with various file types.

When emotional intelligence instruction is included in the curriculum, students became better at solving problems in complex situations involving human emotions. They become better at communicating their emotions and at responding to others with empathy and openness (William Woods University 2021). At the same time, by sharing emotions and helpful personal experiences, including their own strengths and talents, teachers can become role models who communicate a growth mindset to their students and colleagues.

It is important that teachers create an ongoing monitoring system that assesses and evaluates student learning. They also need to feel comfortable asking for feedback and adjusting their teaching accordingly. To continually improve emotional intelligence in their classrooms, teachers need to reflect and ask themselves the following questions:

- What kinds of learning experiences do I offer?
- What opportunities do I provide for my students to have teacher and peer interactions?

- What opportunities do I provide for my students to connect the subject content to real life?
- What opportunities do I provide for my students to connect the subject content to their emotional intelligence?
- How do I augment my students' natural abilities?
- How do I create an effective student-centered classroom?

Mărgăriţoiu (2020) stresses,

[T]oday's online education must take into account more than ever the impact the current context bears on the emotions and feelings of all educational actors-teachers, students, parents, on their willingness and availability to connect and relate. They need to inject their messages with many classifications, encouragement, and problem-solving. They must show understanding, patience, and support and care for everyone in order to emerge, in good conditions, and together, from the social, financial, familial and personal crisis generated by the COVID-19 pandemic. (44)

This sentiment carries over to the present. Good communication adapted to new realities and strong organizational skills are critical for teaching with emotional intelligence.

Support from Policy Work

Teacher training programs that emphasize social-emotional learning and support teachers in managing and lowering their own stress levels are crucial: teachers must look after themselves before taking care of others. Some steps have been taken in this regard.

In response to the COVID-19 pandemic, the US House Appropriations Committee advocated for teachers by proposing an unprecedented $260 million for social-emotional learning as part of the 2020 federal education bill (Committee for Children 2019). As educational monies are allocated to states through grants, support for further federal investment and ongoing bipartisan interest in social-emotional learning are continuing to grow. The committee pointed out that a teacher's mental health influences school and classroom climates, and, because a teacher's emotions are contagious to students, supporting students means first supporting teachers.

In the spring and summer of 2020, organizations such as CASEL and the Yale Center for Emotional Intelligence published resources to help teachers adjust to teaching virtually (Ferren 2020). This was accompanied by a rise in policy options and funding in support of social-emotional education when many school districts were returning to traditional brick-and-mortar schools.

Policy and advocacy work was initiated at both the federal and state levels to address long-standing and emergent needs for social-emotional learning. Posamentier (2021) reported on success working with Congress to include social-emotional learning in COVID-19 relief legislation and the regular budget appropriations cycle. This resulted in historic, dedicated investments in social-emotional learning as well as funding increases through traditional budget negotiations that supported social-emotional learning, including through Title IV-A, Title I, and the Every Student Succeeds Act (Posamentier 2021).

Additionally, material was added to a federal government handbook for school districts instructing schools on how to implement social and emotional learning in remote learning environments; this was used to help meet the potential mental health needs of students returning to face-to-face classes (Posamentier 2021). As recognition of social-emotional learning grows, it is hoped that the voice of advocates will promote a level of discourse that digs deeper and promotes efforts to analyze, strategize, improve, and sustain policy changes.

Implications for the Future

This book has made the case that emotional intelligence can be learned and developed to benefit teaching and learning in a virtual setting. The book identifies the need for teachers not only to understand but to embrace the role of teaching emotional intelligence to students in an online classroom. It underlines the concept that online teachers must learn to manage their own emotions before they can help students regulate their emotions and build relationships with both teacher and peers. The support of online teachers is critical to create a safe, welcoming, and inclusive virtual classroom environment where meaningful learning can take place for all students.

Teacher training in emotional intelligence is vital. Staff development can help online teachers master how to intentionally teach the whole child in order to help students shape and build relationships and to foster trust, respect, and collaboration in a virtual (or a face-to-face) learning environment.

Teachers must carefully, and intentionally, plan opportunities and lessons to impart self-management skills to students and integrate thinking skills into students' decision-making, planning, and self-evaluation experiences. Complex teaching is a prerequisite for complex learning; teachers must deliberately prepare and assess their lessons to help students develop empathy, appreciation, and reflective skills (Folsom 2009). It is the teacher's responsibility to evaluate how well their plans implement these curricular improvements. Teachers should understand that although advanced instruction may take time to implement, developing one's emotional intelligence is an ongoing process that reaps worthwhile benefits. Both teachers and students will become more conscious of learning the skills and habits needed to improve the relationships that are key to their psychological well-being and physical health.

Developing one's emotional intelligence can take a lifetime. However, recognizing the significant impact emotions have on learning and on creating a positive virtual classroom culture can help online teachers lay the foundation for developing their students' self-confidence and well-being. Developing their own emotional intelligence, as well as that of their students, can help teachers become better equipped to prepare students for the future.

Cultivating Emotional Intelligence in Schools

When a school or district includes emotional intelligence in the curriculum, it should communicate with parents to inform them of the purpose and goals, as it would with any curriculum change. By clarifying the benefits of the district's social-emotional learning program, virtual schools can garner parents' support and address any concerns before they become an issue (Prothero 2022).

It is crucial that parents know the connection between academic success and emotional intelligence (Bradberry and Greaves 2009) and that they understand the importance of online teachers incorporating emotional intelligence in their lessons. Emotional intelligence is linked to people being happier, physically healthier, friendlier, more creative, and more willing to take chances (Aguilar 2016, exhibit 6.2), and these are traits many parents would like to see in their children.

In the future, as education becomes increasingly automated, teaching emotional intelligence skills will become even more important. As the education system follows trends in the use of artificial intelligence (AI), online learning systems may foster increasingly independent learning on the part of students. Concerns that AI will lead to teacher and student separation and weaken opportunities to support student emotional intelligence have yet to be realized. Lai et al. (2023) conclude that further research is needed to explore the effects of AI on student emotional and mental development.

Reimagining the Future

When social distancing was a temporarily imposed measure, as during the COVID-19 pandemic, teaching with technology offered a chance to think about transformative change when redesigning the future of education. Education researcher Keith Holmes argues that an online school community can provide insights on how to sustain current relationships, peer-to-peer learning, intellectual engagement, services, and sense of belonging: "Reducing the focus on the physical or virtual environments and increasing the focus on people, and the development of crucial social and emotional skills including empathy and solidarity, could prove a survival strategy for sustaining learning communities through and beyond COVID-19" (Holmes 2020). To ensure the sustainability of virtual teaching as a learning community, intentional effort and commitment are required of all stakeholders—administrators, teachers, parents, and students.

When imagining the future of online education, it is vital to address the threat to the immediate and long-term supply of teachers. The National Foundation for Educational Research found that teaching is one of the most stressful jobs (Gallup 2014). In 2021 nearly one in four teachers reported they were likely to leave their teaching jobs by the end of the 2020–2021 school year (Steiner and Woo 2021). Therefore, support and professional development training are critical to help online teachers identify and manage their emotions so they can create a virtual learning environment that is healthy for both teachers and children and in which all children can learn.

Elevating Success

Connecting Emotional Intelligence to the Online Classroom reveals the transformational influence emotional intelligence has on the purposeful unlocking of a child's academic and social-emotional development in a virtual environment. Emotional intelligence is a critical trait that is relevant for both teachers and students. For teachers, emotional intelligence fosters an ability to understand and help online students identify, label, and manage their emotions effectively while recognizing and empathizing with the emotions of others. For students, emotional intelligence promotes better learning through self-awareness that facilitates making conscious choices in accordance with their personal values and goals. It fosters empathy, builds positive and meaningful relationships, promotes academic success, and offers wider implications for engaging work that leads to future job success.

Research is needed to explore online teachers' attitudes toward supporting emotional intelligence in virtual instruction. Seminars, workshops, and courses for online teacher preparation are necessary if teachers view emotional intelligence as an essential educational pathway for online teaching and learning and want to integrate emotional intelligence into their online curricula.

Because parents play an important role in their child's education, it is important that teachers and parents work together to understand, value, and use emotional intelligence skills with children taught in an online classroom. School districts can provide parents with workshops to increase their awareness and, in this way, build strong ties for communication and parental support.

With the tools presented throughout this book, teachers will be ready to facilitate the development of emotional well-being in themselves and their students. Enjoy the journey!

TEACHING TIP

Question

How can I make my students aware of and help them celebrate their academic as well as social-emotional growth?

Answer

Teachers can ask students to set personal academic goals. These goals can be monitored and shared with the teacher throughout the year. At the end of the school year, students can reflect to determine whether they met their goals and explain why or why not. Teachers can also have each student create a personal timeline of their life in which they record and illustrate meaningful milestones. In this way, students can see all they have accomplished in their life. If they share their timelines with the class, students can discuss the similarities and differences between their timeline and those of others.

References

Acuña, Kym, and Phillip J. Blacklock. 2022. "Mastery Teachers: How to Build Success for Each Student in Today's Classrooms." *Journal of Higher Education Theory and Practice* 22 (1): 136–40. https://doi.org/10.33423/jhetp.v22i1.4970.

Adams, Kimberly S., and Sandra L. Christenson. 2000. "Trust and the Family-School Relationship Examination of Parent-Teacher Differences in Elementary and Secondary Grades." *Journal of School Psychology* 38 (5): 477–97. https://doi.org/10.1016/S0022-4405(00)00048-0.

Agostin, Tracy McKee, and Sherry K. Bain. 1997. "Predicting Early School Success with Developmental and Social Skills Screeners." *Psychology in the Schools* 34 (3): 219–28. https://doi.org/10.1002/(SICI)1520-6807(199707)34:3.

Aguilar, Elena. 2016. *The Art of Coaching Teams: Building Resilient Communities That Transform Schools*. Jossey-Bass.

Albert, Daniel J. 2020. "The Classroom Culture of a Middle School Music Technology Class." *International Journal of Music Education* 38 (3): 383–99. https://doi.org/10.1177/0255761419881483.

Alharbi, Mohammed Abdullah, and Abdulrahman Nasser Alqefari. 2022. "Students' Uptake and Perspectives on Teacher and Peer Feedback on Written Assignments." *Learning and Teaching in Higher Education: Gulf Perspectives* 18 (2): 107–18. https://doi.org/10.1108/LTHE-02-2021-0015.

Armstrong, Patricia. 2010. "Bloom's Taxonomy." Vanderbilt University Center for Teaching. https://cft.vanderbilt.edu/guides-sub-pages/blooms-taxonomy/.

Asih, Pribadi, Herlan Suherlan, Bertha Jean Que, Ira Kusumawaty, Patriandi Nuswantoro, Asrianti Asrianti, and Andiyan Andiyan. 2022. "Online Psychology Education for

Students in the Context of the COVID-19 Pandemic." *Special Education* 1 (43): 2009–18.

Babu, A. Suresh, and Sree R. R. Koduru. 2022. "Understanding Social and Emotional Intelligence Skills Development of Undergraduate Students through Virtual Classes: An Analytical Study." *Language in India* 22 (11): 143–49.

Bali, Maha, and Adham R. Ramadan. 2007. "Using Rubrics and Content Analysis for Evaluating Online Discussion: A Case Study from an Environmental Course." *Journal of Asynchronous Learning Networks* 11 (4): 19–33.

Barbour, Michael K., and Kelly L. Unger. 2014. "Strategies for Overcoming Common Obstacles in the Online Environment: Issues in Virtual School Teaching." In *Real Life Distance Education: Case Studies in Practice*, edited by A. A. Piña and A. P. Mizell, 21–40. Information Age Publishing.

Beeman, Kendall L. 2022. "The Quiet Girl in a Virtual World: Learning from the Virtual Classroom to Better Support Quiet Girls in the Middle Grades." *Research in Middle Level Education Online* 45 (7): 1–19. https://doi.org/10.1080/19404476.2022 .2106082.

Bell, Courtney A., Nathan D. Jones, Yi Qi, and Jennifer M. Lewis. 2018. "Strategies for Assessing Classroom Teaching: Examining Administrator Thinking as Validity Evidence." *Educational Assessment* 23 (4): 229–49. https://doi.org/10.1080/10627197 .2018.1513788.

Boettcher, Judith V., and Rita-Marie Conrad. 2010. *The Online Teaching Survival Guide: Simple and Practical Pedagogical Tips.* Jossey-Bass.

Bonwell, Charles C., and James A. Eison. 1991. *Active Learning: Creating Excitement in the Classroom.* ASHE-ERIC Higher Education Report No. 1. George Washington University School of Education and Human Development. https://files.eric.ed.gov/fulltext /ED336049.pdf.

Boyd, Donald, Pam Grossman, Marsha Ing, Hamilton Lankford, Susanna Loeb, and James Wyckoff. 2011. "The Influence of School Administrators on Teacher Retention Decisions." *American Educational Research Journal* 48 (2): 303–33. https://doi.org/10 .3102/0002831210380788.

Boykin, A. Wade, and Pedro Noguera. 2011. *Creating the Opportunity to Learn: Moving from Research to Practice to Close the Achievement Gap.* ASCD. https://eric.ed.gov/?id =ED524209.

Brackett, Mark A., and Susan E. Rivers. 2014a. "Preventing Bullying with Emotional Intelligence." *Education Week* 33 (21): 32–33. https://www.edweek.org/leadership/opinion -preventing-bullying-with-emotional-intelligence/2014/02.

Brackett, Marc A., and Susan E. Rivers. 2014b. "Preventing Bullying with Emotional Intelligence." *The Conversation*, May 11, 2014. https://theconversation.com/preventing -bullying-with-emotional-intelligence-25992.

Bradberry, Travis. 2023. *Emotional Intelligence Habits: A Powerful New Way to Increase Your Emotional Intelligence*. TalentSmartEQ.

Bradberry, Travis, and Jean Greaves. 2009. *Emotional Intelligence 2.0*. TalentSmart.

Bradley-Dorsey, Martha, Dennis Beck, Robert Maranto, Bich Tran, Thomas Clark, and Feng Liu. 2022. "Is Cyber like In-Person? Relationships between Student-Student, Student-Teacher Interaction and Student Achievement in Cyber Schools." *Computers and Education Open* 3:100101. https://doi.org/10.1016/j.caeo.2022.100101.

Brame, Cynthia J. 2016. "Active Learning." Vanderbilt University Center for Teaching. https://cft.vanderbilt.edu/guides-sub-pages/active-learning/.

Bratsis, Michael E. 2017. "Health Wise: Getting Their Names Right." *Science Teacher* 84 (5): 14.

Brazelton, G. B. 2020. "Online Course Engagement through Relationship Management and Content Creation." *New Directions for Teaching and Learning* 2020 (164): 105–13. https://doi.org/10.1002/tl.20429.

Brigandi, Carla B., Nancy K. Spillane, Karen E. Rambo-Hernandez, and Jana Stone. 2022. "Teaching in the Time of COVID-19: A Biological Systems Theory Approach." *Frontiers in Education* 7. https://doi.org/10.3389/feduc.2022.964492.

Brooks, D. Christopher, and Jeffrey Pomerantz. 2017. *ECAR Study of Undergraduate Students and Information Technology*. EDUCAUSE. https://eric.ed.gov/?id=ED588872.

Cacciatore, Gianna. 2021. "Teacher-Student Relationships Matter." *Usable Knowledge*, March 17. Harvard Graduate School of Education. https://www.gse.harvard.edu/ideas/usable-knowledge/21/03/teacher-student-relationships-matter.

Cavaleri, Michelle, Satomi Kawaguchi, Bruno Di Biase, and Clare Power. 2019. "How Recorded Audio-Visual Feedback Can Improve Academic Language Support." *Journal of University Teaching and Learning Practice* 16 (4): 1–19. https://doi.org/10.53761/1.16.4.6.

Chen, Jie-Qi, Seana Moran, and Howard Gardner. 2009. *Multiple Intelligences around the World*. Jossey-Bass.

Cherry, Kendra. 2023. "Understanding Body Language and Facial Expressions." *VeryWell Mind*, February 23. https://www.verywellmind.com/understand-body-language-and-facial-expressions-4147228.

Chickering, Arthur W., and Zelda F. Gamson. 1987. "Seven Principles for Good Practice in Undergraduate Education." *AAHE Bulletin* (March): 3–6. https://files.eric.ed.gov/fulltext/ED282491.pdf.

Cho, Moon-Heum, and Demei Shen. 2013. "Self-Regulation in Online Learning." *Distance Education* 34 (3): 290–301. https://doi.org/10.1080/01587919.2013.835770.

Clemons, Hank. 2022. "'The Head or Heart' Emotional Intelligence: A Critical Skill for Better Decision Making." Webinar, Training Officers Consortium, June 14. https://www.trainingofficers.org/event/the-head-or-heart-emotional-intelligence-a-critical-skill-for-better-decision-making.

Cole, Michele T., Louis B. Swartz, and Daniel J. Shelley. 2020. "Threaded Discussion: The Role It Plays in E-Learning." *International Journal of Information and Communication Technology Education* 16 (1): 16–29. https://doi.org/10.4018/IJICTE.2020010102.

Collaborative for Academic, Social, and Emotional Learning (CASEL). 2023. "Advancing Social and Emotional Learning." https://casel.org/.

Collins, Lauren W., and Timothy J. Landrum. 2023. "Using Behavioral Interventions to Build Relationships with Students with Challenging Behavior." *Teaching Exceptional Children* 55 (3): 188–97. https://doi.org/10.1177/00400599221085727.

Committee for Children. 2019. "Unprecedented National Gains for Social-Emotional Learning for Both Teachers and Students." *Committee for Children Blog*, June 5. https://www.cfchildren.org/blog/2019/06/unprecedented-national-gains-for-sel-for-teachers-and-students/.

Conklin, Sheri, and Amy Garrett Dikkers. 2021. "Instructor Social Presence and Connectedness in a Quick Shift from Face-to-Face to Online Instruction." *Online Learning* 25 (1): 135–50. https://doi.org/10.24059/olj.v25i1.2482.

Cook, Ruth Gannon. 2023. "Can Dialogic Narratives and Discourse Engage Online Learners?" *Participatory Educational Research* 10 (5): 1–18. https://doi.org/10.17275/per.23.72.10.5.

Cunningham, Bruce, and Alan I. Sugawara. 1988. "Preservice Teachers' Perceptions of Children's Problem Behaviors." *Journal of Educational Research* 82 (1): 34–39. https://doi.org/10.1080/00220671.1988.10885862.

Dabrowski, Joan, and Tanji Reed Marshall. 2018. *Motivation and Engagement in Student Assignments: The Role of Choice and Relevancy*. The Education Trust. https://files.eric.ed.gov/fulltext/ED593328.pdf.

Dâmbean, Camelia Angelica. 2021. "Emotional Intelligence and Communication in Human Resources Management to Avoid Occupational Stress." *Acta Marisiensis: Seria Technologica* 18 (2): 36–41. https://doi.org/10.2478/amset-2021-0016.

Darwish, Aya. 2021. "The Role of Emotional Intelligence in Education and How It Is Linked to Effective Teaching." LinkedIn. https://www.linkedin.com/pulse/role-emotional-intelligence-education-how-lined-teaching-aya-darwish.

David, Susan. 2016. *Emotional Agility: Get Unstuck, Embrace Change, and Thrive in Work and Life*. Penguin Random House.

Davis, Angela C., Cassandra Wright, M. Curtis, M. E. Hellard, M. S. C. Lim, and M. J. Temple-Smith. 2021. " 'Not My Child': Parenting, Pornography, and Views on Education." *Journal of Family Studies* 27 (4): 573–88. https://doi.org/10.1080/13229400.2019.1657929.

Dolighan, Tim, and Michael Owen. 2021. "Teacher Efficacy for Online Teaching during the COVID-19 Pandemic." *Brock Education* 30 (1): 95–116. https://doi.org/10.26522/brocked.v30i1.851.

Dost, Meliha Tuzgöl, Hayrunnisa Aslan, and A Mücahit Aslan. 2022. "Effects of the COVID-19 Pandemic on Students, Teachers, and Parents according to School Counselors' Perceptions" (in Turkish). *Egitim ve Bilim* [Education and Science] 47 (211): 1–25. https://doi.org/10.15390/eb.2022.10508.

Dougherty, Cailyn N., Michelle Parker, Lautrice Nickson, and Casey Creghan. 2022. "The Impact of Student Choice on Reading." *English in Texas* 52 (1): 20–24.

Durlak, Joseph A., Roger P. Weissberg, Allison B. Dymnicki, Rebecca D. Taylor, and Kriston B. Schellinger. 2011. "The Impact of Enhancing Students' Social and eEmotional Learning: A Meta-Analysis of School-Based Universal Inventions." *Child Development* 82 (1): 405–32.

Duzgun, Serkan. 2022. "Exploring Teachers' Views on Emotion Transfer in Virtual Classrooms during Emergency Remote Teaching." *Turkish Online Journal of Distance Education* 23 (4): 1–19. https://doi.org/10.17718/tojde.1182741.

Dweck, Carol. 2006. *Mindset: The New Psychology of Success.* Ballantine Books.

Dwivedi, Alka, Prasoom Dwivedi, Samo Bobek, and Simona Sternad Zabukovšek. 2019. "Factors Affecting Students' Engagement with Online Content in Blended Learning." *Kybernetes* 48 (7): 1500–15. https://doi.org/10.1108/K-10-2018-0559.

Editorial Team of Resilience Educator. 2013. "Daniel Goleman's Emotional Intelligence Theory Explained." Resilient Educator, February 27. https://resilienteducator.com/classroom-resources/daniel-golemans-emotional-intelligence-theory-explained/.

EdTrust. 2021. "The Importance of Strong Relationships between Teachers and Students." Brief, March 17. EdTrust. https://edtrust.org/resource/the-importance-of-strong-relationships/

Ekman, Paul. 1992. "An Argument for Basic Emotions." *Cognition and Emotion* 3 (4): 169–200. https://doi.org/10.1080/02699939208411068.

Ekornes, Stine. 2017. "Teacher Stress Related to Student Mental Health Promotion: The Match between Perceived Demands and Competence to Help Students with Mental Health Problems." *Scandinavian Journal of Educational Research* 61 (3): 333–53. https://doi.org/10.1080/00313831.2016.1147068.

Epstein, Jennifer A., and Judith M. Harackiewicz. 1992. "Winning Is Not Enough: The Effects of Competition and Achievement Orientation on Intrinsic Interest." *Personality and Social Psychology Bulletin* 18 (2): 128–38. https://doi.org/10.1177/0146167292182003.

Esquivel, Paloma. 2022. "Nearly Half of LAUSD Students Have Been Chronically Absent This Year; Data Show." *Los Angeles Times*, March 31. https://www.latimes.com/california/story/2022-03-31/lausd-students-chronic-absent-amid-covid-pandemic.

Fan, Xitao, and Michael Chen. 2001. "Parental Involvement and Students' Academic Achievement: A Meta-Analysis." *Educational Psychology Review* 13 (1): 1–22. https://doi.org/10.1023/A:1009048817385.

Farmer, Dionna. 2020. "Teacher Attrition: The Impacts of Stress." *Delta Kappa Gamma Bulletin* 87 (1): 41–50.

Faulconer, Emily, John Griffith, and Amy Gruss. 2022. "The Impact of Positive Feedback on Student Outcomes and Perceptions." *Assessment and Evaluation in Higher Education* 47 (2): 259–68. https://doi.org/10.1080/02602938.2021.1910140.

Ferren, Megan. 2020. "Social and Emotional Supports for Educators during and after the Pandemic." Center for American Progress. https://www.americanprogress.org/article/social-emotional-supports-educators-pandemic.

Fischer, Kurt W., and Thomas R. Bidell. 2006. "Dynamic Development of Action and Thought." In *Handbook of Child Psychology: Theoretical Models of Human Development*, edited by R. M. Lerner and W. Damon, 313–399. John Wiley and Sons.

Folsom, Christy. 2009. *Teaching for Intellectual and Emotional Learning (TIEL)*. Rowman and Littlefield Education.

Frisby, Brandi N., and Matthew M. Martin. 2010. "Instructor-Student and Student-Student Rapport in the Classroom." *Communication Education* 59 (2): 146–64. https://doi.org/10.1080/03634520903564362.

Fullan, Michael. 2001. *Leading in a Culture of Change*. Jossey-Bass.

Gallup. 2014. *State of America's Schools: The Path to Winning Again in Education*. Gallup.

Garcia, Antero, Aaron Guggenheim, Kristina Stamatis, and Bridget Dalton. 2021. "Glimmers of Care: Attending to the Affective Everyday in Ninth-Grade Literacy Classrooms." *Reading Research Quarterly* 56 (2): 337–54. https://doi.org/10.1002/rrq.296.

Gardner, Howard. 1983. *Frames of Mind: Theory of Multiple Intelligences*. BasicBooks.

Gayton, Jorge, and Beryl C. McEwen. 2007. "Effective Online Instructional and Assessment Strategies." *American Journal of Distance Education* 21 (3): 117–32. https://doi.org/10.1080/08923640701341653.

Gilbert, Patricia K., and Nada Dabbagh. 2005. "How to Structure Online Discussions for Meaningful Discourse: A Case Study." *British Journal of Educational Technology* 36 (1): 5–18. https://doi.org/10.1111/j.1467-8535.2005.00434.x.

Goleman, Daniel. 1995. *Emotional Intelligence: Why It Can Matter More than IQ*. Bantam Books.

Goleman, Daniel. 1998. *Working with Emotional Intelligence*. Bantam Books.

Goleman, Daniel. 2006. *Social Intelligence: The New Science of Human Relationships*. Bantam Books.

Goleman, Daniel. 2023. "The Art of Effective Feedback." Korn Ferry. https://www.kornferry.com/insights/this-week-in-leadership/feedback-performance-management-emotional-intelligence.

Gottman, John. 1997. *Raising an Emotionally Intelligent Child*. Simon and Schuster.

Graziano, Paulo A., Janine Slavec, Rosmary Ros, Leanna Garb, Katie Hart, and Alexis Garcia. 2015. "Self-Regulation Assessment among Preschoolers with Externalizing

Behavior Problems." *Psychological Assessment* 27 (4): 1337–48. https://doi.org/10.1037/pas0000113.

Greenberg, Mark T., Celene E. Domitrovich, Roger P. Weissberg, and Joseph A. Durlak. 2017. "Social and Emotional Learning as a Public Health Approach to Education." *Future of Children* 27 (1): 13–32.

Gupta, Kriti Priya. 2023. "Exploring Student Engagement in Virtual Classrooms: A Person-Centred Approach Using Cluster Analysis." *International Journal of Educational Management* 37 (1): 117–34. https://doi.org/10.1108/IJEM-08-2022-0309.

Händel, Marion, Svenja Bedenlier, Bärbel Kopp, Michaela Gläser-Zikuda, Rudolf Kammerl, and Albert Ziegler. 2022. "The Webcam and Student Engagement in Synchronous Online Learning: Visually or Verbally?" *Education and Information Technologies* 27 (7): 10405–28. https://doi.org/10.1007/s10639-022-11050-3.

Hawthorn-Embree, Meredith L., Christopher H. Skinner, John Parkhurst, Michael O'Neil, and Elisha Conley. 2010. "Assignment Choice: Do Students Choose Briefer Assignments or Finishing What They Started?" *School Psychology Quarterly* 25 (3): 143–51. https://doi.org/10.1037/a0020914.

Hojjati, Nafiseh, and Balakrishnan Muniandy. 2014. "The Effects of Font Type and Spacing of Text for Online Readability and Performance." *Contemporary Educational Technology* 5 (2): 161–74. https://doi.org/10.30935/cedtech/6122.

Holmes, K. 2020. "Sustaining Learning Communities through and beyond COVID-19." *NORRAG Blog*, April 27. https://www.norrag.org/sustaining-learning-communities-through-and-beyond-covid-19-by-keith-holmes/.

Immordino-Yang, Mary Helen. 2008. "The Smoke around Mirror Neurons: Goals as Sociocultural and Emotional Organizers of Perception and Action in Learning." *Mind, Brain, and Education* 2 (2): 67–73.

Immordino-Yang, Mary Helen, Linda Darling-Hammond, and Christina Krone. 2018. *The Brain Basis for Integrated Social, Emotional, and Academic Development: How Emotions and Social Relationships Drive Learning.* The Aspen Institute. https://files.eric.ed.gov/fulltext/ED596337.pdf.

Iqbal, Javed, Naima Qureshi, Muhammad Azeem Ashraf, Samma Faiz Rasool, and Muhammad Zaheer Asghar. 2021. "The Effect of Emotional Intelligence and Academic Social Networking Sites on Academic Performance during the COVID-19 Pandemic." *Psychology Research and Behavior Management* 14:905–20. https://doi.org/10.2147/PRBM.S316664.

Jacobs, Lynette, and Kevin L. G. Teise. 2019. "Educators' Subjective Experiences of Workplace Bullying within a Perceived Neoliberalist Education System." *South African Journal of Education* 39 (4): 1–9. https://doi.org/10.15700/saje.v39n4a1868.

Jones, Stephanie M., and Emily J. Doolittle. 2017. "Social and Emotional Learning: Introducing the Issue." *Future of Children* 27 (1): 3–12.

Jones, Stephanie M., Sophie P. Barnes, Rebecca Bailey, and Emily J. Doolittle. 2017. "Promoting Social and Emotional Competencies in Elementary School." *Future of Children* 27 (1): 49–72. https://www.jstor.org/stable/44219021.

Joyner, Fredricka. 2012. "Increasing Student Interaction and the Development of Critical Thinking in Asynchronous Threaded Discussions." *Journal of Teaching and Learning with Technology* 1 (1): 35–41.

Kemp, Elyria, McDowell Porter III, Nwamaka A. Anaza, and Dong-Jun Min. 2021. "The Impact of Storytelling in Creating Firm and Customer Connections in Online Environments." *Journal of Research in Interactive Marketing* 15 (1): 104–24. https://doi.org/10.1108/JRIM-06-2020-0136.

Kerrigan, John, and Rosa Aghekyan. 2022. "Beyond the Discussion Board: Engaging Students in Asynchronous Online Activities." *International Journal of Teaching and Learning in Higher Education* 33 (3): 488–95.

Kim, Kyung-Sun, and Joi L. Moore. 2005. "Web-Based Learning: Factors Affecting Students' Satisfaction and Learning Experiences." *First Monday* 10 (11). https://firstmonday.org/ojs/index.php/fm/article/view/1294.

Ko, Susan, and Steve Rossen. 2010. *Teaching Online: A Practical Guide.* Routledge.

Koh, Joyce Hwee Ling, and Rebecca Yen Pei Kan. 2020. "Perceptions of Learning Management System Quality, Satisfaction, and Usage: Differences among Students of the Arts." *Australasian Journal of Educational Technology* 36 (3): 26–40. https://doi.org/10.14742/ajet.5187.

Kosslyn, Stephen M. 2021. *Active Learning Online: Five Principles That Make Online Courses Come Alive.* Alinea Learning.

Krcmar, Patricia, and Belinda Dunnick Karge. 2019. "Administrators Supporting Teacher-Student Foster Youth Relationships through Full Utilization of the LCFF & LCAP." *Multicultural Education* 27 (1): 43–52.

Krneta, Ljiljana, and Emina Simunic. 2021. *Encouraging the Emotional Competence of Students in School.* Grafid (Bosnia and Herzegovina).

Kumar, Parul, Neha Kumar, and Hiram Ting. 2023. "An Impact of Content Delivery, Equity, Support and Self-Efficacy on Student's Learning during the COVID-19." *Current Psychology* 42 (3): 2460–70. https://doi.org/10.1007/s12144-021-02053-3.

Lai, Tinghong, Chuyin Xie, Minhua Ruan, Zheng Wang, Hong Lu, and Shimin Fu. 2023. "Influence of Artificial Intelligence in Education on Adolescents' Social Adaptability: The Mediatory Role of Social Support." *PLoS ONE* 17 (3): 1–10. https://doi.org/10.1371/journal.pone.0283170.

Landis, Carter. 2021. "Teachers See Different Hardships during COVID-19." Michigan State University School of Journalism, news release, March 31. https://news.jrn.msu.edu/2021/03/teachers-see-different-hardshi.

Lee, Sang Joon, and Robert Maribe Branch. 2022. "Students' Reactions to a Student-Centered

Learning Environment in Relation to Their Beliefs about Teaching and Learning." *International Journal of Teaching and Learning in Higher Education* 33 (3): 298–305.

Lee, Youngju, and Jaeho Choi. 2011. "A Review of Online Course Dropout Research: Implications for Practice and Future Research." *Educational Technology Research and Development* 59:593–618. https://doi.org/10.1007%2Fs11423-010-9177-y.

Lehrer, Jonah. 2010. *How We Decide*. Mariner Books.

Lengyel, Piroska Szegediné. 2023. "Learning in an Online Environment: Let's Focus on Emotional Awareness." *International Journal of Emerging Technologies in Learning* 18 (4): 219–34. https://doi.org/10.3991/ijet.v18i04.34887.

Lerkkanen, Marja-Kristiina, and Eija Pakarinen. 2021. "Parental Trust in Teachers and Children's Interest in Reading and Math: A Longitudinal Study." *European Education* 53 (3/4): 152–67. https://doi.org/10.1080/10564934.2022.2080562.

Li, Cathy, and Farah Lalani. 2020. "The COVID-19 Pandemic Has Changed Education Forever. This Is How." World Economic Forum, April 29. https://www.weforum.org/agenda/2020/04/coronavirus-education-global-covid19-online-digital-learning.

Li, Han, Robert E. Kraut, and Haiyi Zhu. 2021. "Technical Features of Asynchronous and Synchronous Community Platforms and Their Effects on Community Cohesion: A Comparative Study of Forum-Based and Chat-Based Online Mental Health Communities." *Journal of Computer-Mediated Communication* 26 (6): 403–21. https://doi.org/10.1093/jcmc/zmab016.

Lickona, Thomas. 2021. "8 Ways Parents Can Teach and Get Respect." *Psychology Today* (blog), November 11. https://www.psychologytoday.com/us/blog/raising-kind-kids/202111/8-ways-parents-can-teach-and-get-respect.

Lisenbee, Peggy S., and Carol M. Ford. 2018. "Engaging Students in Traditional and Digital Storytelling to Make Connections Between Pedagogy and Children's Experiences." *Early Childhood Education Journal* 46:129–139. https://doi.org/10.1007/s10643-017-0846-x.

Luca, Joseph, and Pina Tarricone. 2001. "Does Emotional Intelligence Affect Successful Teamwork?" In *Meeting at the Crossroads: Proceedings of the 18th Annual Conference of the Australasian Society for Computers in Learning in Tertiary Education*, edited by G. Kennedy, M. Keppell, C. McNaught, and T. Petrovic, 367–76. University of Melbourne.

Lumpkin, Angela. 2021. "Online Teaching: Pedagogical Practices for Engaging Students Synchronously and Asynchronously." *College Student Journal* 55 (2): 195.

MacMillan, Carrie. 2020. "Why 'Social and Emotional Learning' Is So Important for Kids Right Now." Yale Medicine, news, November 6. https://www.yalemedicine.org/news/social-emotional-child-development.

Mărgăriţoiu, Alina. 2020. "Reconfiguration and a New Type of Teacher-Student Relationship in Online Education." *Jus et Civitas* 2:43–50.

Markic, Olga. 2009. "Rationality and Emotions in Decision Making." *Interdisciplinary Description of Complex Systems* 7 (2): 54–64.

Martin, Florence, and Doris U. Bolliger. 2018. "Engagement Matters: Student Perceptions on the Importance of Engagement Strategies in the Online Learning Environment." *Online Learning* 22 (1): 205–22. https://doi.org/10.24059/olj.v22i1.1092.

McDonald, Anna T. 2021. "The Importance of Cultivating Emotional Intelligence in Schools." *Independent School Magazine*, Spring. https://www.nais.org/magazine /independent-teacher/spring-2021/the-importance-of-cultivating-emotional -intelligence-in-schools/.

McGlynn, Kaitlyn, and Janey Kelly. 2020. "Digging Deeper into Virtual Learning: How to Engage All Students in Science from a Distance." *Science Scope* 44 (2): 90–95.

McKown, Clark. 2017. "Social-Emotional Assessment, Performance, and Standards." *Future of Children* 27 (1): 157–78. https://doi.org/10.1353/foc.2017.0008.

Mérida-López, Sergio, Martin Sánchez-Gómez, and Natalio Extremera Pacheco. 2020. "Leaving the Teaching Profession: Examining the Role of Social Support, Engagement and Emotional Intelligence in Teachers' Intentions to Quit." *Psychosocial Intervention* 29 (3): 141–51. https://doi.org/10.5093/pi2020a10.

Merry, Kevin Luke. 2021. "Developing Emotionally Intelligent Teaching Approaches in Online Learning." *Journal of Perspectives in Applied Academic Practice* 9 (2): 12–15. https://doi.org/10.14297/jpaap.v9i2.472.

Michigan, D. 2020. "How Online Learning Will Change the Education System Post Covid-19." *Entrepreneur, India*, May 27.

Milman, Natalie B. 2020. "Differentiating Instruction in Online Environments." *Distance Learning* 17 (4): 73–76. https://www.proquest.com/openview/de85575b330aab4ac 27f8b1a99d6f25b/1.

Ministerul Educației și Cercetării [Ministry of Education and Research, Romania]. 2020. "Strategia privind digitalizarea educației din România" [Strategy on digitalization of education in Romania]. https://www.edu.ro/sites/default/files/SMART.Edu%20-%20 document%20consultare.pdf.

Minshew, Andy. 2019. "Why Strong Teacher Student Relationships Matter." *Waterford.org* (blog), April 29. https://www.waterford.org/education/teacher-student-relationships/.

Moody, S. M., and S. D. Matthews. 2021. "Skip on Skippyjon: Helping Preservice Teachers Build Anti-Racist Classrooms through Critical Book Evaluations." *Ohio Journal of English Language Arts* 61 (1): 29–34.

Moore, Karol Ann. 2021. "Considering the Emotional Needs of Students in a Computer- Based Learning Environment." *Educational Technology Research and Development* 69 (1): 63–66. https://doi.org/10.1007/s11423-020-09891-1.

Mphahlele, Letebele. 2022. "Students' Perception of the Use of a Rubric and Peer Reviews in an Online Learning Environment." *Journal of Risk and Financial Management* 15 (11): 503. https://doi.org/10.3390/jrfm15110503.

Mugilan, Kalai, Ayanna Sterling, and Carol Vance. 2021. *Emotional Intelligence and Virtual Learning Environments: A Humanistic Approach.* Community Publishing House.

Muhammad, Gholdy E. 2020. *Cultivating Genius: An Equity Model for Culturally and Historically Responsive Literacy.* Scholastic.

Muhammad, Gholnecsar E., Nickolaus A. Ortiz, and Mary L. Neville. 2021. "A Historically Responsive Literacy Model for Reading and Mathematics." *Reading Teacher* 75 (1): 73–81. https://doi.org/10.1002/trtr.2035.

Muirhead, William D. 2000. "Online Education in Schools." *International Journal of Educational Management* 14 (7): 315–24. https://doi.org/10.1108/09513540010378969.

Murphy, Ann, Derek Malenczak, and Mina Ghajar. 2019. "Identifying Challenges and Benefits of Online Education for Students with a Psychiatric Disability." *Journal of Postsecondary Education and Disability* 32 (4): 395–409.

Nevins, Mark. 2020. "Why a Post-Covid World Demands Greater Emotional Intelligence." *Forbes*, September 29. https://www.forbes.com/sites/hillennevins/2020/09/29/why -a-post-covid-world-demands-greater-emotional-intelligence/.

Nguyen, Tiffany, Shayla White, Kenneth Hall, and Reginald Bell. 2019. "Emotional Intelligence and Managerial Communication." *American Journal of Management* 19 (2): 54–63. https://doi.org/10.33423/ajm.v19i2.2068.

Nizielski, Sophia, Suhair Hallum, Paulo N. Lopes, and Astrid Schütz. 2012. "Attention to Student Needs Mediates the Relationship between Teacher Emotional Intelligence and Student Misconduct in the Classroom." *Journal of Psychoeducational Assessment* 30 (4): 320–29. https://doi.org/10.1177/0734282912449439.

O'Connor, Peter J., Andrew Hill, Maria Kaya, and Brett Martin. 2019. "The Measurement of Emotional Intelligence: A Critical Review of the Literature and Recommendations for Researchers and Practitioners." *Frontiers in Psychology* 10.

Osika, Alexandra, Stephanie MacMahone, Jason M. Lodge, and Annemaree Carroll. 2022. "Emotions and Learning: What Role Do Emotions Play in How and Why Students Learn." Times Higher Education, March 18. https://www.timeshighereducation.com /campus/emotions-and-learning-what-role-do-emotions-play-how-and-why-students -learn.

Ounprasertsuk, Jatuporn, and Wanich Suksatan. 2021. "The Effectiveness of an Emotional Intelligence Promotion Program in the Emotional Intelligence of Preschool Children in Kanchanaburi Province." *Systematic Reviews in Pharmacy* 12 (2): 613–17.

Panadero, Ernesto, and Anders Jönsson. 2020. "A Critical Review of the Arguments against the Use of Rubrics." *Educational Research Review* 30:100329. https://doi.org/10.1016 /j.edurev.2020.100329.

Pânişoară, Georgeta, Cristina Ghiţă, Ruxandra Chirca, and Alina Grecu. 2020. "Study on the Differences between Students, Teachers and Parents Regarding the Attendance to Online Courses." *Romanian Journal of School Psychology* 13 (26): 64–71.

Pappas, Christopher. 2015. "The Impact of Emotional Intelligence in eLearning." eLearning Industry, May 20. https://elearningindustry.com/impact-of-emotional-intelligence -in-elearning.

Parrish, Nina. 2018. "How to Teach Self-Regulation." Edutopia, August 22. https://www .edutopia.org/article/how-teach-self-regulation.

Pekrun, Reinhard. 2014. *Emotions and Learning.* International Academy of Education and International Bureau of Education. https://unesdoc.unesco.org/ark:/48223 /pf0000227679.

Peng, Fei, Lili Kang, Jinhai Shi, and Ming Liu. 2023. "Cultural Distance, Classroom Silence and Culturally Responsive and Inclusive Education: Evidences from Migrant College Students in Shanghai." *Behavioral Sciences* 13 (3): 193. https://doi.org/10.3390 /bs13030193.

Penner, Jon G. 1984. *Why Many College Teachers Cannot Lecture: How to Avoid Communication Breakdown in the Classroom.* Charles Thomas.

Pešikan, Ana, Hannele Niemi, and Iztok Devetak. 2021. "Education in the Covid-19 Era." *Center for Education Policy Studies Journal* 11:7–15. https://doi.org/10.26529/cepsj .1306.

Petrides, Kostantinos V., and Adrian Furnham. 2001. "Trait Emotional Intelligence: Psychometric Investigation with Reference to Established Trait Taxonomies." *European Journal of Personality* 15 (6): 425–48. https://doi.org/10.1002/per.416.

Petrova, Petya. 2020. "Modern Challenges in the Application of Personalized Models in Student Education for the Benefit of Business and Society." *Izvestia Journal of the Union of Scientists - Varna, Economic Sciences Series* 9 (3): 88–95. https://doi.org/10.36997 /IJUSV-ESS/2020.9.3.88.

Pink, Daniel H. 2009. *Drive.* Riverhead Books published by Penguin.

Platz, Monika. 2021. "Trust between Teacher and Student in Academic Education at School." *Journal of Philosophy of Education* 55 (4–5): 688–97.

Posamentier, Jordan. 2021. "Empowering SEL through Policy and Advocacy." *Committee for Children Blog,* November 30. https://www.cfchildren.org/blog/2021/11/empowering -sel-with-the-power-of-policy-and-advocacy/.

Powell, Douglas R., Seung-Hee Son, Nancy File, and Robert R. San Juan. 2010. "Parent–School Relationships and Children's Academic and Social Outcomes in Public School Pre-Kindergarten." *Journal of School Psychology* 48 (4): 269–92.

Pozo Rosado, Pablo, Alberto Grao-Cruces, Ester Ayllon-Negrillo, and Raquel Pérez-Ordás. 2022. "Effects on Empathy and Emotional Intelligence of a Teaching Personal and

Social Responsibility Programme in Physical Education." *Retos (Nuevas Perspectivas de Educación Física, Deporte y Recreación)* 44:504–14.

Pressley, Tim, Hannah Croyle, and Madison Edgar. 2020. "Different Approaches to Classroom Environments Based on Teacher Experience and Effectiveness." *Psychology in the Schools* 57 (4): 606–26. https://doi.org/10.1002/pits.22341.

Prior, Jennifer. 2014. "Focus on Elementary: Love, Engagement, Support, and Consistency: A Recipe for Classroom Management." *Childhood Education* 90 (1): 68–70. https://doi .org/10.1080/00094056.2014.872518.

Prothero, Arianna. 2022. "How School Leaders Can Respond to Pushback over Social-Emotional Learning." *Education Week*, April 13. https://www.edweek.org/leadership /how-school-leaders-can-respond-to-pushback-over-social-emotional-learning /2022/04.

Quílez-Robres, Alberto, Pablo Usán, Raquel Lozano-Blasco, and Carlos Salavera. 2023. "Emotional Intelligence and Academic Performance: A Systematic Review and Meta-Analysis." *Thinking Skills and Creativity* 49 (September). https://doi.org/Elsevier. https://www.sciencedirect.com/science/article/pii/S1871187123001244.

Quintana-Orts, Cirenia, Sergio Mérida-López, Lourdes Rey, and Natalio Extremera. 2021. "Closer Look at the Emotional Intelligence Construct: How Do Emotional Intelligence Facets Relate to Life Satisfaction in Students Involved in Bullying and Cyberbullying?" *European Journal of Investigation in Health, Psychology and Education* 11 (3): 711–25. https://doi.org/10.3390/ejihpe11030051.

Rajab, Mohammad H., and Mohammed Soheib. 2021. "Privacy Concerns over the Use of Webcams in Online Medical Education during the COVID-19 Pandemic." *Cureus* 13 (2): 13536.

Raouna, Kyriaki. 2021. "5 Personalized Learning Strategies for the Online Learner." *Getting Smart*, July 12. https://www.gettingsmart.com/2021/07/12/5-personalized-learning -strategies-for-the-online-learner/.

Rathaliya, Aarti, S. Malarkodi, Rupinder Deol, and Rajarajeswari Kuppuswamy. 2022. "Perception, Burden and Satisfaction of Parents of Children Attending Online Classes during COVID-19 Lockdown: A Cross-Sectional Survey." *Journal of Family Medicine and Primary Care* 11 (6): 2493–98. https://doi.org/10.4103/jfmpc.jfmpc_1717_21.

Rawson, Andrew. 2021. "Creating Psychological Safety in a Virtual Environment." Training Industry, July 21. https://trainingindustry.com/articles/strategy-alignment-and -planning/creating-psychological-safety-in-a-virtual-environment/.

Rello, Luz, and Ricardo Baeza-Yates. 2013. "Good Fonts for Dyslexia." In *Proceedings of the 15th International ACM SIGACCESS Conference on Computers and Accessibility, ASSETS 2013*. Association for Computing Machinery. https://doi.org/10.1145 /2513383.2513447.

Rello, Luz, Martin Pielot, Mari-Carmen Marcos, and Roberto Carlini. 2013. "Size Matters (Spacing Not): 18 Points for a Dyslexic-Friendly Wikipedia." In *Proceedings of the 10th International Cross-Disciplinary Conference on Web Accessibility*, 1–4. Association for Computing Machinery. https://doi.org/10.1145/2461121.2461125.

Renzulli, Joseph S., and Carolyn M. Callahan. 2008. "Product Assessment." In *Alternative Assessments with Gifted and Talented Students*, edited by J. L. Van Tassel-Baska. Prufrock Press.

Rio Poncela, Ana María, L. Romero Gutierrez, D. D. Bermúdez, and M. Estellés. 2021. "A Labour of Love? The Invisible Work of Caring Teachers during Covid-19." *Pastoral Care in Education* 39 (3): 192–208. https://doi.org/10.1080/02643944.2021.1938646.

Robin, Bernard R. 2008. "Digital Storytelling: A Powerful Technology Tool for the 21st Century Classroom." *Theory into Practice* 47 (3): 220–228. https://doi.org/10.1080/00405840802153916.

Rolón-Dow, Rosalie. 2005. "Critical Care: A Color (Full) Analysis of Care Narratives in the Schooling Experiences of Puerto Rican Girls." *American Educational Research Journal* 42 (1): 77–111. https://doi.org/10.3102/00028312042001077.

Ruecker, Todd. 2021. "Retention and Persistence in Writing Programs: A Survey of Students Repeating First-Year Writing." *Composition Forum* 46 (Spring). https://compositionforum.org/issue/46/retention.php.

Ruedas-Gracia, Nidia, Crystal M. Botham, Amber R. Moore, and Courtney Peña. 2022. "Ten Simple Rules for Creating a Sense of Belonging in Your Research Group." *PLoS Computational Biology* 18 (12): 1–10. https://doi.org/10.1371/journal.pcbi.1010688.

Ruhl, Kathy L., Charles A. Hughes, and Patrick J. Schloss. 1987. "Using the Pause Procedure to Enhance Lecture Recall." *Teacher Education and Special Education* 10 (1): 14–18. https://doi.org/10.1177/088840648701000010.

Sabila, Annisa Moza, Mahir Pradana, and Muhammad Idris. 2022. "Analyzing the Effectiveness of Online Learning from Students' Perspective." *Educational Administration: Theory and Practice* 28 (4): 61–73.

Salovey, Peter, and John D. Mayer. 1990. "Emotional Intelligence." *Imagination, Cognition, and Personality* 9 (3): 185–211. https://doi.org/10.2190/DUGG-P24E-52WK-6CDG.

Sánchez-Núñez, María Trinidad, Noelia García-Rubio, Pablo Fernández-Berrocal, and José Miguel Latorre. 2020. "Emotional Intelligence and Mental Health in the Family: The Influence of Emotional Intelligence Perceived by Parents and Children." *International Journal of Environmental Research and Public Health* 17 (17): 6255. https://doi.org/10.3390/ijerph17176255.

Santi, Elena Ancuța, Gabriel Gorghiu, and Costin Pribeanu. 2022. "Students' Engagement and Active Participation during the Pandemic." *Informatica Economica* 26 (1): 5–15. https://doi.org/10.24818/issn14531305/26.1.2022.01.

Schonert-Reichl, Kimberly A. 2017. "Social and Emotional Learning in Teachers." *Future of Children* 27 (1): 137–55. https://eric.ed.gov/?id=EJ1145076.

Sederevičiūtė-Pačiauskienė, Živilė, Ilona Valantinaitė, and Vaida Asakavičiūtė. 2022. " 'Should I Turn on My Video Camera?' The Students' Perceptions of the Use of Video Cameras in Synchronous Distant Learning." *Electronics* 11 (5): 813. https://doi.org/10.3390/electronics11050813.

Simorangkir, Lindawati, Agustaria Ginting, Amnita Anda Yanti Ginting, Aprilita Sitepu, Helinida Saragih, Nasipta Ginting, Friska Ginting, and Marcellina Perangin-angin. 2022. "The Relationship of Parents' Emotional Intelligence with Child Abuse Events in Children Aged 6–12 Years during the Pandemic of COVID-19." *HIV Nursing* 22 (2): 674–77. https://doi.org/10.31838/hiv22.02.133.

Singhal, Meghna. 2021. "6 Things Emotionally Intelligent Parents Do Differently: How Emotionally Intelligent Parents Raise Their Children." *Psychology Today,* January 3.

Stavredes, Tina, and Tiffany Herder. 2014. *A Guide to Online Course Design: Strategies for Student Success.* John Wiley and Sons.

Stein, Kirsten L. 2013. "A Qualitative Narrative Phenomenological Study: Parental Perceptions in Choosing Online Educational Classes for Gifted Children." EdD diss., University of Phoenix.

Steiner, Elizabeth D., and Ashley Woo. 2021. *Job-Related Stress Threatens the Teacher Supply.* Rand Corporation. https://www.rand.org/content/dam/rand/pubs/research_reports/RRA1100/RRA1108-1/RAND_RRA1108-1.pdf.

Štibi, Ivana, Mojca Čepič, and Jerneja Pavlin. 2021. "Physics Teaching in Croatian Elementary and High Schools during the Covid-19 Pandemic." *Center for Educational Policy Studies Journal* 11:1–26. https://doi.org/10.26529/cepsj.1135.

Sulistianingsih, Endang, Sanday Jamaludin and Sumartono Sumartono. 2018. "Digital Storytelling: A Powerful Tool to Develop a Student's Emotional Intelligence." *Journal of Curriculum Indonesia* 1 (2): 33–40. https://doi.org/10.15294/JCI.V1I2.3.

Sull, Errol Craig. 2020. "The Beginning Connection in an Online Course: Crucial!" *Distance Learning* 17 (3): 108.

Sutherland, Kevin S., Maureen A. Conroy, Bryce D. McLeod, Rachel Kunemund, and Kim McKnight. 2019. "Common Practice Elements for Improving Social, Emotional, and Behavioral Outcomes of Young Elementary School Students." *Journal of Emotional and Behavioral Disorders* 27 (2): 76–85. https://doi.org/10.1177/1063426618784009.

Suyatno, Suyatno, Dholina Inang, Ganis Amurdawati, Asih Mardati, and Yulia Rachmawati. 2021. "Does Self-Actualization Influence Students' Readiness? A Structural Equation Model Analysis." *Ilkogretim Online* 20 (1): 899–906. https://doi.org/10.17051/ilkonline.2021.01.83.

Tantillo Philibert, Carla, and Allison Slade. 2022. *Everyday SEL in the Virtual Classroom: Integrating Social Emotional Learning.* Routledge.

Thompson, Holly. 2021. "What Is Self-Regulation? 10 Skills and Ways to Improve Them." *Indeed*, September 18. https://www.indeed.com/career-advice/career-development/self-regulation-skills.

Tipper, Christine M., Giulia Signorini, and Scott T. Grafton. 2015. "Body Language in the Brain: Constructing Meaning from Expressive Movement." *Frontiers in Human Neuroscience* 9. https://doi.org/10.3389/fnhum.2015.00450.

Tomlinson, Carol Ann. 1999. *The Differentiated Classroom: Responding to the Needs of All Learners*. Association for Supervision and Curriculum Development.

Tonks, DeLaina, Royce Kimmons, and Stacie L. Mason. 2021. "Motivations among Special Education Students and Their Parents for Switching to an Online School: Survey Responses and Emergent Themes." *Online Learning* 25 (2): 171–89. https://doi.org/10.24059/olj.v25i2.2141.

Turner, Kristen Hawley, and Ivelisse Ramos Brannon. 2022. "Connections Matter: Building Engagement in Online Learning Spaces." *English Education* 54 (2): 108–27. https://doi.org/10.58680/ee202231753.

Uddin, Lucina Q., Marco Iacoboni, Claudia Lange, and Julian Paul Keenan. 2007. "The Self and Social Cognition: The Role of Cortical Midline Structure and Mirror Neurons." *Trends in Cognitive Sciences* 11 (4): 153–57. https://doi.org/10.1016/j.tics.2007.01.001.

Uysal, Funda, and İmgehan Elgün. 2022. "Examining the Learning Outcomes of the Teaching Principles and Methods Course in the Context of Student-Centered Learning." *Sakarya University Journal of Education* 12 (2): 327–43. https://doi.org/10.19126/suje.1050680.

Vega, Vanessa. 2012. "Social and Emotional Learning Research Review." Edutopia, November 7. https://www.edutopia.org/sel-research-learning-outcomes.

Vejayaratnam, Navaratnam, Azlina Haron, Nor Hafizah Mohammad Hanafi, and Nor Lailatul Azilah Hamdzah. 2023. "Learners in Blended Environments: Emotional and Cognitive Intelligence." *Journal of Pharmaceutical Negative Results* 14 (2): 2565–76. https://doi.org/10.47750/pnr.2023.14.02.314.

Villarreal-Davis, Christina, Teri Ann Sartor, and Lauren McLean. 2021. "Utilizing Creativity to Foster Connection in Online Counseling Supervision." *Journal of Creativity in Mental Health* 16 (2): 244–57. https://doi.org/10.1080/15401383.2020.1754989.

Vinovskis, Maris A. 2019. "History of Testing in the United States: PK–12 Education." *Annals of the American Academy of Political and Social Science* 683 (1): 22–37. https://doi.org/10.1177/0002716219839682.

Vlasova, Helen. 2022. "Online Education Statistics—How COVID-19 Changed the Way We Learn?" Admissionly, March 21. https://admissionly.com/online-education-statistics.

Vygotsky, Lev S. 1978. *Mind in Society: The Development of Higher Psychological Processes*. Harvard University Press.

Walkington, Candace, and Matthew L. Bernacki. 2020. "Appraising Research on Person-alized Learning: Definitions, Theoretical Alignment, Advancements, and Future Directions." *Journal of Research on Technology in Education* 52 (3): 235–52. https://doi.org/10.1080/15391523.2020.1747757.

Warmuth, Kelly A., and Alexandria H. Caple. 2022. "Differences in Instructor, Presenter, and Audience Ratings of PechaKucha and Traditional Student Presentations." *Teaching of Psychology* 49 (3): 224–35. https://doi.org/10.1177/00986283211006389.

Watkins, S. Craig. 2009. *The Young and the Digital: What the Migration to Social Network Sites, Games, and Anytime, Anywhere Media Means for Our Future.* Beacon Press.

Watson, Firm Faith, Marianne Castano Bishop, and Debra Ferdinand-James. 2017. "Instructional Strategies to Help Online Students Learn: Feedback from Online Students." *TechTrends: Linking Research and Practice to Improve Learning* 61 (5): 420–27. https://doi.org/10.1007/s11528-017-0216-y.

Weaver, Melanie R. 2006. "Do Students Value Feedback? Student Perceptions of Tutors' Written Responses." *Assessment and Evaluation in Higher Education* 31 (3): 379–94. https://doi.org/10.1080/02602930500353061.

Webber, Amber. 2020. "Emotionally Intelligent Online Teaching: Leading Distance Learners through Uncertainty." *Insider* (Florida International University Online), March 24. https://insider.fiu.edu/emotional-intelligence-online-teaching/.

Westerberg, Diana, Rebecca Newland, and Julia L. Mendez. 2020. "Beyond the Classroom: The Protective Role of Student–Teacher Relationships on Parenting Stress." *Early Childhood Education Journal* 48 (5): 633–42. https://doi.org/10.1007/s10643-020-01024-w.

Wildi-Yune, Jeanny, and Carlos Cordero. 2015. *Corporate Digital Learning: How to Get It "Right."* Position Paper. KPMG. https://assets.kpmg.com/content/dam/kpmg/pdf/2015/09/corporate-digital-learning-2015-KPMG.pdf.

Wilkins, Stephen, Muhammad Mohsin Butt, Joe Hazzam, and Ben Marder. 2023. "Collaborative Learning in Online Breakout Rooms: The Effects of Learner Attributes on Purposeful Interpersonal Interaction and Perceived Learning." *International Journal of Educational Management* 37 (2): 465–82. https://doi.org/10.1108/IJEM-10-2022-0412.

William Woods University. 2021. "Teaching Emotional Intelligence as Part of the Curriculum." *Look into Education* (blog), July 28. https://education-blog.williamwoods.edu/2021/07/teaching-emotional-intelligence-as-part-of-the-classroom-curriculum/.

Wood, Carol. 2017. "Teacher Health and Wellness." *Committee for Children Blog*, July 11. https://www.cfchildren.org/blog/2017/07/teacher-health-wellness-fostering-student-achievement-supporting-teachers-mental-physical-well/.

Wortha, Franz, Roger Azevedo, Michelle Taub, and Susanne Narciss. 2019. "Multiple Negative Emotions during Learning with Digital Learning Environments: Evidence on

Their Detrimental Effect on Learning from Two Methodological Approaches." *Frontiers in Psychology* 10. https://doi.org/10.3389/fpsyg.2019.02678.

Wu, Jiani. 2020. *20 Day Active Listening Challenge in the Virtual Classroom: Practical Strategies to Cultivate Effective Communication and Engage with Your Learners More than Ever!* JW Consulting.

Xiang, Dan, Guihua Qin, and Xiaowei Zheng. 2022. "The Influence of Student-Teacher Relationship on School-Age Children's Empathy: The Mediating Role of Emotional Intelligence." *Psychology Research and Behavior Management* 15:2735–44. https://doi.org/10.2147/PRBM.S380689.

Xiangming, Li, Xuejin Zhang, Xiaoling Zeng, and Jingshun Zhang. 2022. "Exploring Online Student Engagement Scaffolded by Teacher Management Communication Style." *International Journal of Emerging Technologies in Learning* 17 (15): 4–15. https://doi.org/10.3991/ijet.v17i15.31513.

Yale Center for Emotional Intelligence. 2022. "Yale Center for Emotional Intelligence (YCEI)." http://ei.yale.edu.

Yaşlıca, Erdal. 2020. "Sanal Sınıf Ortamında Etkileşimli Öğretim Materyalinin Başarıya ve Tutuma Etkisi" [The impact of interactive teaching material on success and attitude in virtual classroom environment]. *Anadolu University Journal of Social Sciences* 20 (1): 39–56. https://doi.org/10.18037/ausbd.700328.

Yazıcıoğlu, Tansel, and Vedat Aktepe. 2022. "Identifying the Values to Be Acquired by the Students in Inclusive Classrooms Based on the Views of the Classroom Teachers." *International Journal of Progressive Education* 18 (1): 52–64.

Zarifsanaiey, Nahid, Zahra Mehrabi, Sara Kashefian-Naeeini, and Ramlee Mustapha. 2022. "The Effects of Digital Storytelling with Group Discussion on Social and Emotional Intelligence among Female Elementary School Students." *Cogent Psychology* 9 (1): 1–16. https://doi.org/10.1080/23311908.2021.2004872.

Zhang, Yijing, and Ji-Kang Chen. 2023. "Emotional Intelligence and School Bullying Victimization in Children and Youth Students: A Meta-Analysis." *International Journal of Environmental Research and Public Health* 20 (6): 4746. https://doi.org/10.3390/ijerph20064746.

Zhao, Ying, Yong Guo, Yu Xiao, Ranke Zhu, Wei Sun, Weiyong Huang, Deyi Liang, et al. 2020. "The Effects of Online Homeschooling on Children, Parents, and Teachers of Grades 1–9 during the COVID-19 Pandemic." *Medical Science Monitor: International Medical Journal of Experimental and Clinical Research* 26:925591. https://doi.org/10.12659/MSM.925591.

Zilka, Gila Cohen. 2021. "Attitudes, Emotions, and the Use of Emoji in Social Networking Apps by Children, Adolescents, and Young Adults." *Interchange* 52 (3): 337–55. https://doi.org/10.1007/s10780-021-09439-z.

Zorkić, Tijana Jokić, Katarina Mićić and Tünde Kovács Cerović. 2021. "Lost Trust? The Experiences of Teachers and Students during Schooling Disrupted by the Covid-19 Pandemic." *Center for Educational Policy Studies Journal* 11:1–24. https://doi.org/10 .26529/cepsj.1150.

Index

academic achievement, 1, 2; EI-based, 152; parental goals for, 95; parental influence on, 27; performance gaps, 88–89, 123, 140; SEL-based, 13–14, 16; student goals for, 153; student-teacher relationship and, 16

accessibility: of audio and video recordings, 22, 23, 113; communication-based, 116; feedback about, 120; in instruction, 114–16; of the learning environment, 112; tools for, 112; webinar-based, 113

accommodations, 111–21, 120–21, 146; challenges in, 119–20; feedback about, 119, 120; flexibility in, 116–19; in instructions for assignments, 114–16

active learning, 2–4, 38, 43–44, 123–24, 133–34; chat-based, 32, 62–64, 66; definition, 37, 58; discussion threads and, 67, 69; goals and expectations, 53, 54–55, 95; online applications–based, 67, 69, 75; parental influence on, 100, 102; parent-teacher conferences and, 99; peer relationships and, 34, 67, 84; role of technology in, 48, 49, 65, 69, 123–24; school relationships

and, 33–34; student feedback in, 69–72; student intrapersonal issues and, 133–34; student-teacher relationship and, 33–34, 67; tracking in, 78, 124; webcam use and, 46, 65; in webinars without webcams, 48

active listening, 11, 18, 40, 43, 103

Acuña, Kym, 134

advocacy, 124–26, 126–27, 149

aggression, 6, 132

altruism, 11

anxiety, 8; bullying and, 6, 144–45; causes of, 6, 8, 60, 76, 85–86, 96, 144–45; during first webinar, 31; in parents, 96, 97, 104; social, 112

Arnstein, Karen, 133

artificial intelligence (AI), 151

assessment, of online learners: feedback component, 88–91; formative, 76–79, 86, 91; hands-on activities in, 83–84; monitoring systems, 146, 147; by peers, 87; of products, 92; resources for, 82–83; rubrics-based, 86–88; rules and regulations affecting, 80–82; skills taxonomy and, 74–75;

assessment, of online learners (*cont.*)
social-emotional, 91; student choice in, 79–80, 81; summative, 76–77, 79–80. *See also* grades and grading systems

assignments, 59; accommodations for, 117–18, 119; completion timelines, 117–18, 119; instructions for, 114–16; learning expectations and, 75; pacing of, 124; personalization, 55–56, 79–80, 81, 85–86; problems in completion of, 117–18, 119, 134–35; reminders about, 76; school district–based criteria for, 132; stressful, 85–86; student choice of, 65–66, 79–80, 81, 133

assistive applications and technology, 111–12

asynchronous learning, 3, 53, 54, 118; accommodations for, 118; collaborative, 69; communication in, 27, 66–67; definition, 39; formative assessments, 77–78; icebreaker activities, 28, 29, 30; LMS-based, 39, 65, 69; student engagement in, 58–59, 65, 66–67, 69, 78

Athena's Advanced Academy, 23, 87, 88

autonomy, 52, 54, 90, 102, 103, 115, 131, 134

Azevedo, Roger, 7

Babu, A. Suresh, 4

behavior issues, 7, 28, 59, 134, 144–45; assignment completion issues, 134–35; in chat rooms, 63, 72; interventional protocols, 126–27; parents' role regarding, 52–54, 130; relation of EI to, 6, 7, 13, 17, 139; relation of SEL to, 13, 139; relation to stress, 145; self-regulatory behavior, 8–9, 43, 71, 72; student-teacher relationship and, 139; teacher's modeling behavior and, 38, 59, 71–72, 111, 126, 126, 142. *See also* bullying; rules and expectations

Bernacki, Matthew L., 41–42

Blacklock, Phillip J., 134

Black students, 140

blended classrooms, 1

Bloom's Revised Taxonomy, 74–75

body language, 7, 10–11, 12, 40, 47, 140–41, 147

Boettcher, Judith V., 17–18, 24, 67–68, 89

Bolliger, Doris U., 76, 86

Botham, Crystal M., 70

Brannon, Ivelisse Ramos, 70–71

breakout groups and rooms, 29, 60–61, 81

breaks, 118–19, 123

bullying, 6, 110, 144–45

Butt, Muhammad Mohsin, 61

Callahan, Carolyn M., 92

CASEL. *See* Collaborative for Academic, Social, and Emotional Learning

chat and chat rooms, 32, 33, 48, 73, 76, 81, 113, 116, 141; parental involvement, 102; staying on topic, 72–73; as student engagement platform, 62–63

classroom climate, 19–21, 144–45, 149

classroom culture, 20, 39, 47, 52, 53, 55, 126, 127; breakout rooms and, 60; class participation and, 84; communication within, 31, 86; creation, 19, 20, 28, 31–32, 47, 53, 54, 55, 69; inclusivity, 40, 44, 49, 115; learning-focused, 34; product assessments and, 92; self-regulation-based, 43; student polls and, 64; students' engagement with, 53, 60, 64, 67, 72, 75–76, 124; student-supportive, 19, 86; supportive of EI, 146–48; trust-based, 35; as welcoming environment, 59, 111, 127, 150. *See also* behavior issues

classroom participation, 48, 134; assessments of, 75, 84, 124; in chat rooms, 32, 62–63; in group work, 131–32; missed classes,

117; student choice in, 67; student-teacher relationship and, 33–34, 67

clubs, parent-student-teacher, 105–6

coaches, emotional, 100–101, 103, 147

cognitive ability and skills, 78; Bloom's Taxonomy of, 74–75; EI, 146

cognitive development, 45

cognitive quality, of classroom instruction, 43–44

cohesiveness, of classroom community, 31–32, 38, 51–52

collaboration, 22, 122, 124, 129, 133, 150; in breakout rooms, 61; communication-based, 18, 22, 35; in group work, 61–62, 129; online applications–based, 69, 81–82; in parent-teacher relationship, 18, 22, 101–3, 105–6; in PE research design, 41–42; trust-based, 35; wiki use in, 69, 81–82

Collaborative for Academic, Social, and Emotional Learning (CASEL), 13, 143–44, 149

Collins, Lauren W., 51

communication, parent-teacher, 17, 18, 19–23, 24, 26–28, 95, 97–99; communication logs, 106; impact of COVID-19 pandemic on, 138–39; individualized, 98; students' inclusion in, 84–85, 90–91, 99. *See also* emails, parent-teacher

communication, student-teacher, 7, 31, 51, 129, 141, 148; accessibility in, 114–16; in asynchronous learning, 27, 66–67; body language in, 7, 10–11, 12, 40, 47, 140–41, 147; classroom culture and, 34, 86, 122; in group work, 129, 130–32; impact of COVID-19 pandemic on, 138–39; modes and criteria, 21–23; nonverbal, 10–11, 140–41; nonviolent, 7; parental involvement, 102; personalized, 34–35, 59; prior to and during first webinar, 28, 31, 32, 33;

recordkeeping in, 21–22; relation to EI, 16–17; synchronous, 27; teacher's communication style, 20, 32; teaching strategies for, 19–25; trust-based, 18, 34–35; with younger students, 36, 76. *See also* emails, student-teacher

compassion, 1, 5, 7, 24, 59, 101, 141, 143

competition, effects on motivation, 10

comprehension, assessment of, 75–76, 77, 122, 124

conflict management, 8–9, 17, 39, 51, 71, 145; in group work, 130, 131, 132–33

Conklin, Sheri, 20, 22, 25, 32, 34, 39, 114

connectivity, in online learning and teaching, 51–52, 145–46; chat box–based, 32, 33; communication-based, 17, 19; during COVID-19 pandemic, 138–39; empathy-based, 17–18; initial connections for, 19, 26–31; for parents, 17, 19–20, 103–6; in parent-teacher relationship, 103–6; among students, 21; in student-teacher relationship, 15–25, 47; through visual recordings, 48. *See also* student-teacher relationship

Conrad, Rita-Marie, 17–18, 24, 67–68, 89

Conroy, Maureen A., 34

Cook, Ruth Gannon, 66–67

cooperation, 11, 56

cooperative learning, 38

Cornell University, 12

course content and structure, 43–45

COVID-19 pandemic, 2, 3, 4–5, 15, 34, 42, 138–39, 144, 148–49, 151–52

creativity, 1, 3, 7, 79, 81, 82, 87, 144, 151

critical thinking, 26, 37, 67, 75, 87, 128, 143

cultural factors, in parental EI, 101

cultural sensitivity, 44, 49, 115, 128–29

curriculum, 56; EI integration into, 139, 143, 146–47, 151, 152–53; emotional learning

curriculum (*cont.*)
    models, 143–45; goals, 54–55; modifications, 55, 90, 151; parental criticism of, 102–3; standards-based, 74; student feedback on, 70–71, 90; teacher's autonomy over, 54
cyberbullying, 6, 126

Darwish, Aya, 3
decision-making, responsible, 13, 80, 147, 150; about accommodations, 119; about class participation, 43; cultural and social context, 128; about development of interests, 45; effect of emotions on, 12, 144; feedback about, 95; parental, 93; about peer interactions, 43, 56; self-awareness-based, 8; about student responsibility, 143
Dikkers, Amy Garrett, 25
discussion groups, parent and parent-teacher, 105–6
distance learning, 3
dyslexic students, 115, 120

education: automation of, 151; goals, 37–38; standards, 80–81
educational teams, 17–18
e-learning, 3
emails, parent-teacher, 24, 54, 76, 90–91, 105, 116; documentation of, 21–22; frequency and scheduling of, 20, 22, 97–98
emails, student-teacher, 23, 34–35, 39, 53, 81, 99, 130, 135; accessibility and, 116; as assignment instruction method, 114; as assignment reminders, 76, 86; effect on student-teacher relationship, 25–26; for empathy building, 18; in group work, 130–31; parental inclusion in, 90–91, 102
emojis, 48, 63–64
emotional distancing, 141–42
emotional expression, 5

emotional intelligence (EI): components, 145; connection to online teaching, 145–46; definition, 5–6; habits for, 145; impact of online learning on, 141–42; impact on learning, 1, 6, 146, 151, 152; parental impact on, 51; students' opinions on, 4; supportive teaching strategies for, 146–48; teachers' facilitator role in, 2–3; teacher training in, 125, 152–53
emotions: identification of, 7, 10–12, 140–41, 146, 152; impact on learning, 7, 141–42; interpretation of, 10–12, 140–41; labeling of, 9, 43, 101, 108, 144, 152; negative, 7, 52, 94, 141, 145; parental, 94; positive, 7, 94; responsibility for, 9; triggers for, 9, 146; validation of, 11, 94, 101; vicarious experience of, 16. *See also specific emotions*
empathy, 6, 7, 8, 17–19, 56, 151–52; in communication, 18–19; in delivery of feedback, 89; in group work, 129; parental, 100; parental influence on, 94; parent-child, 100, 101; parent-teacher, 18, 100, 101, 103; in problem-solving, 11, 101, 1270; promotion of, 56; role of listening in, 66; student-student, 56, 129; student-teacher, 10–11, 18–19, 25, 64–65, 66, 89, 146
Every Student Succeeds, 149
exercise, 10

face-to-face learning: comparison with online learning, 4; student-teacher relationship in, 140; teaching style for, 47; transition from online learning to, 1, 15, 125, 138–39, 149; transition to online learning from, 138
facial expressions, 7, 47, 140–41
feedback: parent-teacher, 69–70, 90–91, 95, 98, 119; student-student, 56, 89–90
feedback, student-teacher, 10, 56, 62, 69–72, 90–91, 95, 119, 147; with EI, 88–89;

emojis-based, 63; empathy in, 89; with
exit cards, 71; during first webinar, 31–32;
influence on student engagement, 134;
influence on student-teacher relationship, 59; negative, 88–89; rubrics-based,
86–88; soliciting of, 69–72, 120, 147; video
recordings-based, 48, 106

forums, virtual, 66; icebreaker activities,
28–29; prompts in, 28, 67–68; questions
in, 28–29, 81; single- *vs.* multiple-question,
81. *See also* threaded discussions

Frankel, Valerie, 116

Frisby, Bradi N., 33–34

games / gamified learning, 41, 62, 73, 117, 124,
147; for formative assessment, 78–79;
parental involvement, 103

Gardner, Howard, *Theory of Multiple Intelligence,* 50, 127

gender issues, 49, 115

gifted students, 87, 119

Goleman, Daniel, EI framework, 6, 8–13, 40,
89, 142–43, 145. *See also* empathy; motivation; self-awareness; self-regulation, social
skills

grades and grading systems, 82, 89, 119;
rubrics, 86–88

group dynamics, of classroom community,
31–32, 33. *See also* cohesiveness

group work: accommodation in, 118; assessments in, 81–82, 84; breakout rooms in,
60–61; collaboration in, 61–62, 129;
communication in, 129, 130–32; conflict
management in, 130, 131, 132–33; instructions for, 114; wiki use in, 81–82

growth mindset, 89, 138, 142–43, 144, 147

hands-on learning, 15, 83–84, 123–24

Hazzam, Joe, 61

hearing-impaired students, 111–12

Hill, Andrew, 91

Holmes, Keith, 151–52

homeless students, 140

homeschooled students, 117, 119–20

homework policies, 24, 106, 108–9

humor, 20, 50

hybrid learning, 3, 58, 138, 139

icebreaker activities, 28–30, 31, 33; in group
work, 130

Immordino-Yang, Mary Helen, 16

inclusivity and diversity, in the virtual classroom, 40, 44, 49, 68, 115, 128–29. *See also*
accessibility; accommodations

individualized education plans, 111

individual learners, support for, 55–56

in-person learning. *See* face-to-face learning

intelligence, intrapersonal, 76, 127

interests, of students, 41, 47, 50–51, 68, 80

internet, 30, 96, 113, 135–36; lost/unstable
connections, 113, 127

interpersonal issues, in online learning, 127–33

interpersonal relationships: assessment of,
74–75; impact of COVID-19 pandemic on,
140; impact on learning, 33–34; negative
effect of online learning on, 142; skills for,
13, 56, 143–44. *See also* parent-teacher
relationship; student-student relationship;
student-teacher relationship

interventional protocols, 126–27

intrapersonal issues, in online learning, 76,
133–36, 144

introductory activities, in webinars, 28–32, 33

journaling, 9, 10, 71, 147

Kaya, Maria, 91

Kenton, Fran, 37

Kimmons, Royce, 110
Koduru, Sree R. R., 4
Koehler, Jessica, 122
Koessler, Katie, 138
Krneta, Ljiljana, 7
Kunemund, Rachel, 34

Landrum, Timothy J., 51
Latino students, 140
leadership, 12, 24, 56, 60, 72, 147
learning: auditory, 124; COVID-19 pandemic
    interruption of, 140; emotion-based dis-
    parities, 111–12; goals in, 97, 110; impact
    of EI on, 1, 6, 146, 151, 152; impact of
    emotions on, 7, 141–42; impact of student-
    teacher relationship on, 33–34, 139, 145–46;
    independent, 102; inquiry-based, 147;
    kinesthetic, 124; visual, 124. See also active
    learning; online learning; social and emo-
    tional learning (SEL)
learning communities, 126, 151–52
learning differences and styles, 46, 124;
    accommodations and adaptations for,
    111–12, 113, 119, 133–34, 147; group work
    and, 118
learning environment: accessibility, 112;
    emotions as component of, 7; in the home,
    103–4; individual students' needs in, 85;
    parent-teacher relationship and, 26; posi-
    tive, supportive, and welcoming, 18–26,
    37, 47, 59, 111, 122, 131; student-centered,
    124. See also fact-to-face learning; online
    learning; virtual classroom
learning levels, 87, 133–34
learning management systems (LMSs), 34,
    39, 53, 97; accessibility issues, 112, 115;
    assessment applications, 81–82; classroom
    individualization with, 65; definition, 39;
    parent-teacher communication in, 97–98,

102, 106; recordkeeping features, 78;
    special-needs students and, 120; text-chat
    areas, 113; threaded discussions in, 48;
    wikis in, 81–82
Lengyel, Piroska Szegediné, 16
lifelong learning, 37–38
listening skills, 7, 119, 145; active listening, 11,
    18, 40, 43, 103; attentive listening, 12;
    supportive listening, 56
LMSs. See learning management systems

Măgăriţoiu, Alina, 148
Marcus, Megan, 42
Marder, Ben, 61
Martin, Brett, 91
Martin, Florence, 76, 86
Martin, Matthew M., 33–34
Mason, Stacie L., 110
Mayer, John D., 5–6
McKnight, Kim, 34
McKown, Clark, 91
McLeod, Bryce D., 34
mentoring, 102, 105
message groups, 76
messaging, 116
metacognition, 37
Milbert, Sydney Miller, 1
mindfulness, 9, 31, 33, 103
Moore, Amber R., 70
motivation, 6, 7, 8, 11, 124, 125–26, 146, 147;
    effects of competition on, 10; extrinsic and
    intrinsic, 9–10, 79; lack or loss, 18, 45, 85;
    motivational quality, 43–44; parental in-
    fluence on, 27; student-teacher relationship
    and, 16, 27, 67; teacher strategies for, 11
Muhammad, Gholdy E., 128

names and personal information: of stu-
    dents, 18, 28, 59, 64–65, 68, 73, 84, 107,

113, 135; of students' parents, 18, 98; of
teachers, 96
Nandor, Valerie, 93
Narciss, Susanne, 7
National Foundation for Educational Research, 152
neurodivergent students, 28, 29–30, 32, 112
newsletters, 98, 105
Nichols, Alice, 110

O'Connor, Peter J., 91
office hours, virtual, 21, 24, 59, 102, 159
online learning: challenges in (for students),
4, 38, 127–37, 133–34; challenges in (for
teachers), 4–5, 38, 122–27; comparison
with face-to-face learning, 4; future of,
151–52; government funding of, 148–49;
pace of, 4; parental concerns about, 94–95,
104, 151; parental preferences for, 110–11;
rise of, 3–4; role of EI in, 6; teachers' lack
of experience in, 4–5, 15; teaching skills
required for, 138–43. *See also* asynchronous
learning; synchronous learning
optimism, 64, 142–43

paraphrasing technique, 40
parents: concerns about online learning,
94–95, 104, 151; EI of, 95–97, 100–101,
153; as emotional coaches, 100–101, 108;
emotional lack of control, 94; expectations
about child's education, 99–100, 125; influence on child's EI, 51, 96–97, 100–101;
parenting styles, 93–94, 95–96; preferences
for online learning, 110–11; roles in online
learning, 135–36, 146, 151, 153; video
tutorials for, 106
parent-teacher relationship, 19, 26–28, as
collaboration/partnership, 18, 22, 101–3,
105–6; conferences, 91, 98–99; establishment of, 19–20, 99–100; negative, 27; stress
within, 27, 99, 125; trust within, 18, 20–21,
27, 94–95. *See also* communication, parent-
teacher; feedback, parent-teacher
peer relationships. *See* student-student
relationships
peer teaching, 38
Peña, Courtney, 70
performance/learning gaps, 88–89, 123, 140
personal development, 13–14
personal information. *See* names and personal
information
personality and temperament, 5, 7
personalization, in online learning, 14, 16,
22, 40–42, 45, 78; of assessments, 78; of
communication, 18, 22, 59; inclusivity
in, 68; of learning environment, 124; of
prompts, 67–68, 81; in student-teacher
relationship, 32, 40–42, 47; of student
work and assignments, 55–56, 79–80, 81,
85–86; of webinar background, 47
photographs, 30, 44, 49–50, 82, 107, 115
Pink, Daniel, 9
polls and polling, 30, 59, 62, 64, 69–70, 78–79
privacy, liability, and safety issues, in online
learning, 50, 94–95, 135–36; chat box
participation, 32; parental concerns about,
93, 95, 135; psychological safety, 52;
webcam use, 46, 112, 113. *See also* names
and personal information
problem-solving, 52, 94, 124, 133, 138, 147,
148; empathy in, 11, 101, 127; in group work,
129, 131; parental involvement, 101, 105;
parental role in, 101, 102; self-regulation-
based, 43; student choice in, 41
professional development, 5, 11, 15, 150, 152
professional learning communities, 126
prompts, 78, 117–18; personalization of,
67–68, 81; short list, 30; for student

prompts (*cont.*)
connectivity, 28; student-created, 81; in threaded discussions, 66–67
public speaking, 84, 85–86, 99

questionnaires, 54, 69–71, 76, 99, 131
questions and questioning, 21, 24, 76; about students' interests, 41; in assessments, 75, 77–78, 81, 82; in chat rooms, 62; close-ended, 78, 79; in course content development, 13, 45; in critical thinking, 128; in empathy development, 12; for feedback, 69–71, 90, 95; in icebreaker activities, 28–30; in identification of emotions, 141; for learning accommodations, 119; open-ended, 13, 78; in parent-teacher communication, 19, 21, 95, 99, 102, 105; in problem-solving, 138; for promotion of EI, 1, 146–47; recordings of, 124; in self-awareness development, 8; in self-regulation skills development, 43; single- *vs.* multiple-question format, 81, 99; in slide presentations, 62; for student engagement promotion, 48, 59; in student-teacher communication, 116; for supporting individual students, 55, 56. *See also* polls and polling; surveys

recordings, audio and video, 45, 65, 92, 117, 136; accessibility, 22, 23, 113, 116, 118; as feedback method, 48; of student class participation, 124
Renzulli, Joseph S., 92
report cards, whole-child, 100
Riethmeier, Becky, 118
role models, teachers as, 38, 59, 71–72, 111, 126, 142
rubrics, 86–88
Ruedas-Gracia, Nidia, 70
RULER program, for EI, 144–45

rules and expectations, for online learning, 24–25, 33, 52–54, 57; for assessments, 80–82; for classroom culture, 31–32, 47, 53, 72, 75–76, 86; as self-regulation basis, 39–40; students' role in, 31–32, 53–54; supportive of EI, 57

safety issues. *See* privacy, liability, and safety issues
Salovey, Peter, 5–6
scavenger hunts, 147
school-family-community partnerships, 144
screen readers, 112
SEL. *See* social and emotional learning
self-awareness, 6, 10, 36, 43, 45, 100, 119, 128, 143, 145, 146, 152; in breakout rooms, 61; as CASEL skill set component, 13, 144; in class participation, 56; classroom rules–based, 53; as decision-making basis, 12; definition, 8; developmental models, 143, 144; feedback about, 95; journaling-based, 35–36; parental influence on, 100; in question-asking, 75; as self-regulation skill, 43; in student-student relationships, 128; in student-teacher relationships, 59; teacher strategies for, 9; as TIEL skill set component, 144
self-confidence, 116, 142, 150; academic performance gaps and, 89; choices-based, 80; for class participation, 62–63, 84; cognitive quality–based, 43–44; feedback and, 89; parental influence on, 99, 103, 106; student-teacher relationship–based, 35, 145–46; teachers' lack of, 5
self-esteem, 50, 89, 103
self-harm, 127
self-management. *See* self-regulation
self-reflection, 21, 38, 75, 87–88, 90, 132, 142, 143

self-regulation, 8–9, 45, 71, 85, 91, 103, 108, 119, 142, 146, 152; as CASEL model component, 13, 144; classroom culture and, 39–40; classroom environment and, 39–40, 43; definition, 8, 43; feedback about, 95; lack of, 9; mindfulness-based, 9, 31, 33, 103; negative emotions and, 7; parental influence on, 100; rules-based, 39–40; as self-management, 13, 56, 61, 145, 150; social skills–based, 11–12, 17; teacher strategies for, 10

self-talk, positive, 10

silent presentations, 92

simulation, 38

Simunic, Emina, 7

slide presentations, 41, 44, 49–50, 62, 92, 115, 121

social ability, 74–75

social and emotional learning (SEL), 1, 2, 6, 8, 16, 151–52; assessment of, 87, 91; benefits of, 13–14, 139; CASEL framework, 143–44, 149; in course content, 45; obstacles to, 11; parental role in, 95, 97, 98, 100; policy and advocacy work for, 148–49; teacher's influence on, 139; teacher training in, 148–49, 150

social awareness, 13, 43, 45, 100, 145

social competence, 145

social intelligence, 11

social media, 18, 115–16; age-appropriateness of, 22, 35; parent groups on, 105; professional learning communities, 126; student work postings on, 107; teachers' information on, 96; in teacher-student communication, 22

social neuroscience, 16

social skills, 6, 11–13, 16, 21, 129, 144–45, 146

specialists, educational, 107

special-needs students, 110, 111, 119, 120. See also accessibility; accommodations

speech-to-text tools, 116

Stein, Emma, 58

Stein, Patrick, 74

storytelling, digital, 28, 68–69, 128

stress / stress management, 43, 80, 103; in first webinar, 31; in group work, 129–30, 132–33; in interpersonal relationships, 6, 42; optimism and, 142–43; in parent-teacher relationship, 27, 99; public speaking anxiety, 85–86; in student-teacher relationship, 42, 122–23, 144–45; in teachers, 139–40; webcam use and, 46

struggles, of online learners, 139; accommodations for, 111-12; in online communications, 26; in group work, 132-33; trust-based responses to, 35; webinar recordings and, 113

student choice, in online learning, 102, 110, 147; in assessments, 79–80, 81; in assignments, 65–66, 79–80, 81, 118; in classroom participation, 67; in learning materials selection, 116–17; in sharing of work, 84–85; values- and goals-based, 152

student engagement. See active learning

student-student relationships, 5, 34, 39, 40, 50, 56, 61, 119, 150; in breakout rooms, 60–61; cultural and social context, 128–29; EI-based, 6; establishment prior to initial webinar, 28–30; feedback within, 89–90; impact on learning, 33–34, 146; interpersonal issues in, 127–33; parental concerns about, 104

student-teacher relationship, 1, 2, 5, 6, 42; as caring relationship, 25, 42, 56, 59; collaboration in, 18; communication in, 20–21, 34–36, 140–41; connectivity in, 47; establishment of, 19–20, 42, 50–51, 140, 150;

student-teacher relationship (*cont.*)
feedback in, 88–91, 120, 124; impact of COVID-19 pandemic on, 138–39; impact on learning, 33–34, 139, 145–46; negative effect of online learning on, 142; negative impact of virtual learning on, 4, 15, 142; online tools for, 17–18; parental concerns about, 104; personalization, 32, 40–42, 47, 59; phases, 50–51; student interpersonal issues and, 127–33; student intrapersonal issues and, 133–36; teacher advocacy in, 126–27; as teacher-student-parent relationship, 99–100; trust within, 25–26, 27, 34–35, 42, 45, 51

student work: accessibility of, 116; online posting of, 107; personalization, 55–56; shared with classmates, 84–85. *See also* assignments

surveys, 14, 59, 62, 69–70, 90–91, 141–42

Sutherland, Kevin, 34

syllabus, 24–25, 75

synchronous learning, 3, 45–46, 58; formative assessments in, 77, 78; LMS-based, 39; parent-teacher communication in, 27; webcam use in, 45–46

Taub, Michelle, 7

teachers: authority of, 19–20; EI of, 75, 122–23, 124–26; emotional intelligence (EI) of, 125, 139–41, 150; facilitator role, 1, 2; lack of experience in online teaching, 4–5, 15; personal appearance, 32, 47; professional expectations for, 122–23; role-modeling behavior, 38, 59, 71–72, 111, 126, 142; self-advocacy, 124–25; tone of voice, 10–11, 32, 47–48; work engagement levels, 124–26; working conditions and workload, 68, 122–23, 125–26. *See also* parent-teacher relationship; student-teacher relationship

teaching tips / teacher strategies, 1-2; for academic goals, 153; for accommodations in learning, 110, 120-21; for assignment non-completion, 136-37; for chat room behavior, 72-73; for classroom rules, 57; for emotional connectivity, 35-36; for empathy, 12; for growth mindset, 138; for homework policies, 108-9; for motivations, 11; for parental involvement, 93, 108-9; for positive learning environments, 37; for self-awareness, 9, 35-36; for self-regulation, 10; for social skills, 13; for student choice, 74, 92; for student engagement, 58; for student-student relationships, 122; for student surveys, 14; for transition to online learning, 1, 15

technical issues, in online learning, 5, 24, 139; communication skills, 26; difficulty with computer screen, 112, 120–21; free online resources, 83; internet connection, 113, 127; student access to technology, 82–83, 123; technical vocabulary use, 115; technology in active learning, 48, 65. *See also* webcams

tests and testing: quizzes, 82; standardized, 80. *See also* assessment, of online learners

texting, 97

threaded discussions, 48, 54, 66–67, 69, 81, 82, 90

TIEL model, of emotional learning and thinking, 143–44

time management, 43; deadlines, 147; in group work, 129–30

time sensitivity, 123

Title I, 149

Title IV-A, 149

Tonks, DeLaina, 110

trust: within parent-teacher relationship, 18, 20–21, 27, 94–95; within student-teacher relationship, 25–26, 27, 34–35, 42, 45, 51

Turner, Kristen Hawley, 70–71
twice-exceptional students, 112, 119

US House Appropriations Committee, 148–49

values, alignment with goals, 10
videos: inappropriate, 117; tutorials for
    parents, 106; video conferencing, 97.
    See also recordings, audio and video
Vinovskis, Maris A., 80
virtual classrooms: definition, 39–40; goal,
    38. *See also* online learning
visually impaired students, 112, 115, 120–21
voice recognition software, 112
Vygotsky, Lev, 45

Walkington, Candace, 41–42
webcams, 32, 45–47, 112; absence of, 47–48,
    49, 65; students' reactions to, 58
webinars, 15; captioning tools, 111–12;
    content, 49–50; definition, 39; EI in, 33;

environment, 45–50; initial, 28–33; parental presence during, 102–3; student age
factors, 46; students' acclimation to, 22;
students' inability to attend, 118; virtual
backgrounds, 46–47; with webcams, 46–47,
112; without webcams, 47–48, 49, 65;
whiteboards, 61–62; younger students'
participation, 123–24. *See also* breakout
rooms
welcome letters, 22, 23, 40
Wessling, Suki, 82
whiteboards, 61–62
Wi-Fi access, 123
wikis, 69, 81–82
Wilkins, Stephen, 61
Wortha, Franz, 7

Yale Center for Emotional Intelligence, 144,
    149

zone of proximal development, 45

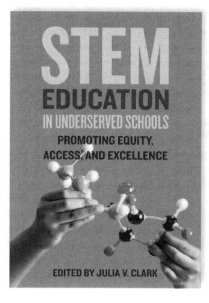
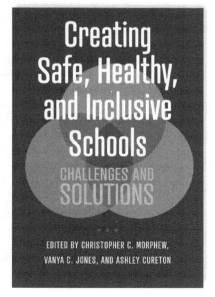
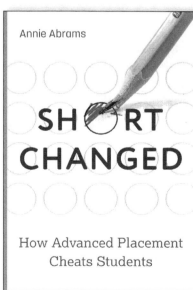